W9-APN-615

DATE DUE

OCT 1 0 1987

APR

TWAYNE'S WORLD AUTHORS SERIES

A Survey of the World's Literature

FRANCE

Maxwell A. Smith, University of Chattanooga

EDITOR

Voltaire

TWAS 583

Voltaire

VOLTAIRE

By PEYTON RICHTER
Boston University
and ILONA RICARDO
Massachusetts Institute of Technology

TWAYNE PUBLISHERS

A DIVISION OF G. K. HALL & CO., BOSTON

Copyright © 1980 by G. K. Hall & Co.

Published in 1980 by Twayne Publishers,
A Division of G. K. Hall & Co.
All Rights Reserved

Printed on permanent/durable acid-free paper and bound
in the United States of America

First Printing

Library of Congress Cataloging in Publication Data

Richter, Peyton E.
Voltaire.

(Twayne's world authors series ; TWAS 583 : France)
Bibliography: p. 179–86
Includes index.
1.   Voltaire, François Marie Arouet de, 1694–1778—
Criticism and interpretation.   I.   Ricardo, Ilona,
joint author. II.   Title.
PQ2122.R48   848′.5′09   79–24985
ISBN 0–8057–6425–9

Contents

About the Authors

Peyton Richter is a professor of Humanities at Boston University who holds a doctorate in philosophy and comparative literature from Duke University. He has also taught at Florida State University and Northeastern University. He is editor of *Perspectives in Aesthetics: Plato to Camus; Utopias: Social Ideals and Communal Experiments,* and *Utopia/Dystopia* and co-editor of *Team Teaching at the College Level* and *Philosophy Looks to the Future: Confrontation, Commitment and Utopia.* A world traveler as well as a photographer and journalist, Professor Richter spent the summers of 1977 and 1979 in France, Switzerland, and Germany visiting and photographing sites associated with Voltaire, Rousseau, Madame de Stael, and Goethe.

Ilona Ricardo received her M.A. and Ph.D. degrees in Romance Languages and Literatures from Harvard University. Her doctoral thesis was on Le Sage. She has taught at Massachusetts Institute of Technology, Northeastern University, and Harvard University. She has translated literary works from Dutch, French, and German into English. Her translations from Gustav Fechner and Jean-Marie Guyau were included in *Perspectives in Aesthetics: Plato to Camus.* She has also written for *Diderot Studies* and *Ungar's Encyclopedia of World Literature.* Her experience in journalism, broadcasting, and the theatre has been extensive. Currently she is studying the techniques of acting in the eighteenth century.

Foreword

Before taking up the subject which has been assigned me, I think it is my duty to warn you about this fellow Voltaire. He has a way of engaging the attention of his devotees to the point where they can think and talk of nothing else. To listen to them, one could hardly avoid the impression that Voltaire's activities are all-embracing; his interests extend to the uttermost ends of human existence; his thought concerns all the topics usually found in an encyclopedia or a dictionary of ideas. Some of this thought is admittedly superficial, but much of it is said to be very profound, and it is not easy to distinguish what is superficial and what is profound. Since Voltairians in general have the same difficulties as non-Voltairians, this constant debate usually ends in a curious compromise: either we decide that Voltaire's ideas are silly, but he is often profound, or that Voltaire, though personally silly, has very profound ideas. When challenged to give specific cases of this philosophical confusion, Voltaire's followers will babble the most nonsensical things imaginable which are only their own beliefs and have but little to do with Voltaire or with you and me. Therefore, we are satisfied to affirm that "so it is, if you think so," or that famous statement of the literary critic Fontenelle, Voltaire's more or less contemporary, who only missed being a centenarian by one month: "Everything is true, and everybody is right."

Let me descend to a few specific examples. Let me cite myself as one of the least important. By 1965, I had had my career, forty years of which had been devoted to Voltaire with some picayune, inconsequential articles. They were, if inconsequential, fairly numerous. In addition, I had written a small book entitled *Voltaire and Candide,* conceived of as an everlasting dialogue between a creator and his created work of art. You see, I had let myself be bitten by the Voltaire bug. Since 1965, I have had to scurry to keep out of jail and the poorhouse. I have taught "Voltaire and his Time" in some dozen American universities and written great big books that nobody can or even wants to read. This is, I suspect, a rather mad world, but, fortunately, there are a lot of sane people in it.

As you can easily see, I hope, I am not a very good example of Voltairian madness. But I once had an undergraduate student at Princeton named Mr. Bessire, who elected to write his senior thesis upon Voltaire. He also visited Ferney, Voltaire's chateau near Geneva, and by scaling the wall surrounding it and giving the *gardien* a handsome tip got a complete tour of the place including the little church that Voltaire had built and dedicated in his name to God. When Mr. Bessire completed his thesis, his concluding sentence was: *Divine Voltaire, ora pro nobis* ("Divine Voltaire, pray for us"). He really was bitten by that Voltaire bug.

If you think we are pretty badly off with this voltairitis, let me cite an even more serious case. I once absentmindedly introduced my friend, the late Theodore Besterman, a well-known Voltairian scholar who had recently founded a Voltaire institute in the *philosophe's* own former residence in Geneva, to some students of mine as "Monsieur de Voltaire." Pleased as Punch, he accepted the introduction by saying: "I live in his house, I sleep in his bed, I publish his correspondence—what would be more natural?"

I suspect that few have been worshiped and adulated more than Voltaire by a larger number of admirers and pseudo-followers. Nor has there been a writer of such eminent distinction in France or Western Europe who has been so savagely hated by an equally large number of critics. The first result of this curious phenomenon of unbalanced judgment is to make a balanced view of his worth hard to come by. It is intriguing that during the horrors of the French Revolution gangs would roam the streets of Paris singing an anthem detailing these horrors to which was attached the refrain: "It is the fault of Voltaire! It is the fault of Rousseau!"

Such antics, however, add but little to our understanding of the meaning of Voltaire. Nor does it help very much, in my humble opinion, to imitate Goethe's laudatory method in referring to Voltaire's excellence by merely giving a string of nouns: "Profundity, genius, intuition, greatness," and so on. Nor does it do much good, either, to call Voltaire "the greatest writer of all

Foreword

time, the most astonishing creation of the author of nature." But, curiously enough, I do think that something is added to Voltaire's worth by that remark made by the scholar Gustave Lanson: "He has given us our freedom and prepared our justice." I wonder why? I also wonder why this present little book written by two of my close Voltairian friends, one of them a student of mine at Harvard, keeps reminding me of Lanson's own little book on Voltaire. Is it because of its judiciousness, its lucidity, or its obvious sincerity? In any case, I like it!

IRA O. WADE

Princeton, New Jersey
January, 1979

Preface

Anyone familiar with the life and works of Voltaire will understand the difficulties we have encountered in trying to fit a comprehensive discussion of so vast a fund of material into so small a space. Dr. Theodore Besterman estimated that about fifteen million of Voltaire's written words survive today, enough to make twenty *Bibles*. Yet we have been presumptuous enough to take their measure and the measure of the man who wrote them in less than two hundred pages. We now understand all too well why Professor Ira Wade once declined an invitation to write a brief book on Voltaire when he discovered that brevity in that case meant *less than seven hundred pages*. This really is a brief book on Voltaire, and we only hope that readers will take it for what it is intended to be: a succinct and highy selective introduction to one of the world's most prolific authors.

We are grateful to Professor Wade for his continual encouragement and for providing us with such a Voltairian foreword, a sort of *facétie* in itself. We also wish to thank for various acts of kindness and assistance Professors Otis Fellows and Jean Sareil of Columbia University, Professor Mary Gegerias of Pine Manor College, Professor Vera Lee of Boston College, and Mrs. Jacqueline Swain of Boston University. To Professor Norman Torrey we express our appreciation for a helpful conference. Finally, Mr. Charles Wirz, *Conservateur* of the Voltaire Institute and Museum in Geneva was very accommodating in providing opportunity for one of us (P.R.) to do research in his institution during the summer of 1977. Working there in Voltaire's own "Les Délices," surrounded by Voltairian memorabilia, was inspirational as well as informative.

We have now finished our book, but as Professor René Pomeau reminds us all, we have not yet finished with Voltaire.

PEYTON RICHTER
ILONA RICARDO

Boston, Massachusetts

Chronology

1694 François Marie Arouet born in Paris, November 21.
1701 Death of his mother.
1704 Admitted to Louis-le-Grand, Jesuit collège in Paris.
1711 Leaves college; studies law; joins Society of the Temple.
1713 In Holland as secretary to French ambassador; love affair with Huguenot girl; sent home to Paris.
1714 Supposedly studying law in Paris and later near Fontainebleau.
1715 Louis XIV dies; Philippe d'Orleans becomes regent for under-aged Louis XV; Arouet returns to Paris.
1716 Forced to go into exile because of works distasteful to Regency; resides with Duke of Sully at Sully-sur-Loire.
1717 Imprisoned in Bastille; assumes name of Voltaire.
1718 Released from prison; his *Oedipus* produced in Paris.
1720 New play, *Artémire*, opens and fails.
1722 Death of father; receives inheritance; pensioned by the king; visits Holland with Mme de Rupelmonde; writes *The Epistle to Urania*; quarrels with the lyric poet Jean-Baptiste Rousseau.
1723 Back in Paris. Publishes first version of *The Henriade* entitled *The League*. Has smallpox. Regent dies. Louis XV becomes king.
1725 *Mariamne* and *The Indiscreet One* produced at court; pensioned by new queen; quarrels with nobleman de Rohan.
1726 Imprisoned in Bastille; upon release embarks for England.
1727 Received by King of England; attends Newton's funeral; meets important literary figures; publishes *Essay on Epic Poetry*.
1728 *The Henriade* published in England, dedicated to English queen.
1729 Returns to France.
1730 His tragedy *Brutus* produced; writes poem *The Death of Mademoiselle Lecouvreur*.

Middle Span

1731 *History of Charles XII* published.
1732 *Zaïre* a great success when produced in Paris.
1733 *The Temple of Taste.*
1734 Publication of his *Philosophical Letters*; flees Paris; settles at Cirey with Mme du Châtelet. Writes a *Treatise on Metaphysics* (unpublished).
1735 Returns to Paris. *The Death of Caesar* produced.
1736 *Alzire* a success in Paris; begins correspondence with Frederick the Great; goes to Holland; writes *The Man of the World.*
1737 Back in Cirey.
1738 *Elements of Newton's Philosophy; Discourses in Verse on Man.*
1740 First meeting with Frederick at Clèves.
1742 *Mohammed* performed in Paris; creates controversy and closes.
1743 *Mérope* a great success in Paris.
1745 Appointed Royal Historiographer to Louis XV; *The Poem of Fontenoy*; death of his brother; *The Temple of Glory.*
1746 Becomes member of the French Academy.
1747 *Zadig;* flees from court with Mme du Châtelet to Sceaux; visits court of King Stanislaus at Lunéville.
1748 *Sémiramis* performed.
1749 Death of Mme du Châtelet.
1750 *Orestes.* Goes to reside at Potsdam in court of Frederick.
1751 *The Age of Louis XIV* published.
1752 *The Diatribe of Doctor Akakia; Poem on Natural Law; Micromégas.*
1753 Leaves Prussia; arrested with niece, Mme Denis, at Frankfurt.
1754 Arrives in Geneva.
1755 Buys "Les Délices"; writes *Poem on the Lisbon Earthquake.*
1756 *Essay on Customs.*
1757 Quarrels with Genevan authorities; resumes correspondence with Frederick of Prussia.
1758 Arranges to purchase estate at Ferney in France near Geneva.
1759 *Candide; History of a Good Brahmin.*
1760 *The Scotch Girl;* quarrels with Jean-Jacques Rousseau.
1761 *Letters on the New Eloise;* erects church at Ferney.

Chronology

1762   Jean Calas executed; *Sermon of the Fifty; The Maid.*

1763   *The Age of Louis XV* published; *Treatise on Tolerance.*

1764   *Jeannot and Colin; Discourse on the Welches; Philosophical Dictionary.*

1765   Calas' name cleared; Voltaire defends Sirven family.

1766   Executions of La Barre and Count de Lally; *The Ignorant Philosopher.*

1767   *The Ingénu.*

1768   Quarrel with Mme Denis who leaves for Paris; *The Princess of Babylon; The Man with Forty Crowns.*

1769   Mme Denis allowed to return to Ferney.

1771   Sirven cleared.

1772   *Questions on the Encyclopedia; Epistle to Horace.*

1774   Louis XV dies; Louis XVI becomes King; *The White Bull.*

1775   *History of Johnny; Lord Chesterfield's Ears.*

1776   *The Bible Finally Explained.*

1778   Voltaire returns to Paris; sees *Irène* performed; dies May 30.

CHAPTER 1

His Greatest Masterpiece: Voltaire's Life

I *Introduction*

FEW men of letters have been so honored and reviled, so praised and maligned as François-Marie Arouet, better known to us as Voltaire.[1] Poet, dramatist, critic, historian, teller of tales, essayist, and pamphleteer, this most conspicuous philosopher of the French Enlightenment projected an image among his contemporaries that evoked as much adulation as it did hostility. As a mere adolescent he charmed prominent French nobles with his irreverent verses and lively wit, and high society eagerly opened its doors to him. But when lackeys of a titled adversary treacherously beat him up not one of his aristocratic friends came to the rescue. Still a young man, he won glory as the author of France's first national epic; yet part of that very epic had been written behind bars.

Controversial to the end, he was hailed by some as the "Confucius of Europe," the "Magistrate of Mankind," while others denounced him as a threat to public morality and legal authority. Proclaimed by his countrymen as the worthy successor of Sophocles, courted by crowned heads, he was nevertheless exiled for most of his adult life from Paris, city of his birth and center of all cultural activities. Intellectual ruler of Europe during his last twenty years, he never ceased to fear pursuit by the French police, and lived close to the Swiss border in case flight might become a necessity. On his final visit to Paris he was idolized by the public, but shortly after his death there his corpse had to be smuggled out of the city by night and buried far away. Even later his physical remains were to be either revered or desecrated, depending upon the politics of changing regimes.

If the circumstances of his life and death were capricious, so were the fortunes of his literary works. His once-renowned epic poem, *The Henriade*, is today forgotten. His numerous plays, which his contemporaries ranked with those of Racine and Corneille, are seldom if ever revived. With the exception of *Candide* and some of his other stories, which remain as popular as ever, the bulk of his enormous literary output is unknown and unappreciated by today's reading public.

Through the years Voltaire's reputation has waxed with the resurgence of revolutionary consciousness, and waned with the reassertion of conservatism. To this day he remains a perennial subject of discussion. Was he, as some claim, a brilliant thinker and original artist, or, as others argue, only a propagandist and popularizer? A closet revolutionary or a closet reactionary? A leader of the avant-garde or a camp follower? A true philosopher or a shifty sophist? Angel of light or prince of darkness? And for today, a historical relic or a still relevant sage?

Only a study of Voltaire's own writings, to which this short book is at most a preface, can help the reader answer these questions. But to understand fully the nature of these writings, we must first have some knowledge of Voltaire the man and of his life, which has been called his greatest masterpiece.[2] While to speak of a man's life as a work of art is to speak metaphorically, in the case of Voltaire's life it seems quite appropriate. In structure his life certainly resembles a drama with its exposition, conflicts and complications, turning points, climax, and *dénouement*. It involves a fascinating but flawed protagonist who struggles mightily to perfect and display his abilities, and to overcome all obstacles to personal fulfillment and happiness. It has its love interests, its passionate friendships, and implacable enmities. Its dialogue is brilliant, its scenario rich in comic and tragic events. Its settings are varied and glamorous, ranging from remote country *châteaux* to royal courts. Its hero learns from his experiences, achieving insight and wisdom with the passing years. As a hero in his own life drama Voltaire resembles his greatest fictional creation Candide. Both heroes are caught up in the continuous turmoil of human existence; both have to overcome ceaseless adversity before they find a modicum of happiness; and, above all, both, in the end, assume responsibility for creating their own existence, for cultivating their own garden.

As we follow the course of Voltaire's life, however briefly, we will be constantly struck by the vitality and versatility of the

man. He was both a writer *and* a man of action; to him the two
were synonymous. He moved from place to place, from idea to
idea, from genre to genre, from one role to another, in his quest
for new experiences and new modes of creative expression. Eventually his life becomes more than just the story of one man's
search for truth and happiness: it is the story of an entire age's
search for enlightenment.

II *The Making of a Poet (1694–1713)*

The most astonishing fact about Voltaire's life is that he lived
it at all. But the puny and half-dead infant delivered to Marie-
Marguerite Daumard, wife of François Arouet, Parisian notary,
on November 21, 1694, managed somehow to survive and to
"enjoy bad health" for eighty-three more years.[3] As a frail
youth he would become a confirmed hypocondriac. As a
withered sage he would nurse the flame of life to its last flicker.

The Arouets were basically bourgeois, though the Daumards
were a provincial family recently elevated to the lesser nobility.
The bright and buoyant mother died when her last-born was
only seven, leaving him with a sister, Marguerite-Catherine, and
a brother, Armand. The sister young François-Marie adored; the
brother, who grew up to be a religious fanatic, he tolerated. The
elder Arouet considered both his sons a little crazy, the elder "in
prose," and the younger "in poetry."

Little is known about the blossoming poet's relations with his
father, although he seems to have respected and loved him in his
own fashion. Sometimes the youth fantasied himself to be the
illegitimate son of a family friend, a minor poet and nobleman.[4]
But he was certainly like his bourgeois father in his respect for
money and social position, and he later managed to get enough of
both to make his life secure and comfortable. He had an inborn
knack for making business deals, even when they seemed contrary
to his philosophy. Along with a poetical heart, he had a cool practical head that some day would make him one of the wealthiest
men in Europe.

To ensure that his youngest son had every opportunity for
advancement, the ambitious notary sent him at the age of ten to
Louis-le-Grand, a fashionable boarding school run by the Jesuits.
The boy might not be the son of a nobleman, but there he could
associate with noblemen and form friendships that would be use-

ful to him in later life.[5] During the seven years that Voltaire spent
at the Jesuit school he got a thorough grounding in the classics.
The good fathers recognized and rewarded his talents for poetry,
theater, and history. He made a number of friends who would
later become influential and be of help to him. But as to religious
indoctrination the school failed miserably. The boy's wit prevailed over piety. He would later remark that his formal education at Louis-le-Grand consisted of "Latin and nonsense," but he
would always remain on good terms with his old teachers and be
grateful to them for forming his taste on the classics. An implacable foe of the Jesuits he certainly later became, but he
always retained some admiration for the love of learning and the
dedication to teaching that the Jesuit fathers at Louis-Le-Grand
had manifested.

During this formative period of his life, however, the Jesuits
were not his only teachers. Worldly hedonists as well as Christian
ascetics were to make their contribution to his education. The
boy's pleasure-loving godfather, the Abbé de Châteauneuf, took
him in hand at the age of twelve and introduced him to a circle
of freethinkers known as the Society of the Temple.[6] He also introduced the youth to his supposed mistress, the aged and cultured courtesan Ninon de Lenclos, who was so impressed with
young Arouet that upon her death she left him money with which
to buy books. The witty and talented boy felt very much at home
in such company. He delighted in the lackadaisical spirit of the
elderly noblemen and ecclesiastics, who met regularly to eat,
drink, and make merry with light verse. In their company there
was no talk of guilt, sin, or repentance. They lived happily in the
present without regret over the past or fear of the future. Their
only religious doctrines consisted in loving life and making the
best of it as long as they could savor the pleasures of the palate
and of poetry. These revellers encouraged the youth in his poetical aspirations. They gave him an appreciative audience for his
wit and histrionics. They refined his taste upon the finest classical
models. He was either too wise or too frail to be led astray by
some of their excesses.

By the time he was ready to leave school he had made up his
mind. He wanted to be a poet, "a man of letters." Informed of
this intention, his bourgeois father reacted as expected. After
trying to argue his son out of following such a parasitic profession

and urging him to follow a more lucrative career in law, the elder Arouet realized that he could not move the stubborn youth. So he packed him off to Holland in the service of the new French ambassador there. It was fall, 1713.

Young Arouet enjoyed the change of scene and was stimulated by the Dutch spirit of freedom and tolerance, so different from that of his native country. But his stay there was soon cut short when his father heard he was having an affair with a Huguenot girl in The Hague. Old Arouet summoned him home immediately, forcing him to leave behind his tearful "precious Pimpette." It was his first love, which he had innocently thought would last forever.

III   *Winning Fame and Notoriety (1714–1726)*

After returning from Holland in December, 1713, young François-Marie consented to study law for a while in order to appease his irate father. As a legal apprentice he spent far more time writing poetry and associating with pleasure-lovers such as Nicolas-Claude Thieriot, a fellow apprentice, than he did pouring over law books. He was still determined to make his way in the world and to become a man of letters. After all, as he bragged, "in leaving the cradle, I stuttered in verse." [7] He had the talent, the willpower, and the urge to be a poet. "I am a man of sensibility," he later confessed, "and nothing but that." [8] The times were ripe for a young man such as he—witty, pleasure-loving, ingratiating, ambitious, and reckless. With the death of old King Louis XIV in 1715, an age of rather tarnished grandeur gave way to an era of frantic hedonism. The reins of government passed to Philip, Duke of Orleans, as Regent for the five-year-old heir to the throne, Louis XV. The Regent's many virtues did not include self-restraint. His unbridled gratification of his lusts set the whole nation a bad but popular example of how to make the most of life while it lasted. The Regent soon burned himself out and died of debauchery, but in the meantime it was a rare and exuberant time in which to be alive and young. François-Marie made the most of it. Already his keen eye for satirical possibilities had begun to focus sharply on the social landscape. In chirping light verse he gleefully ridiculed practically everyone, regardless of wealth, sex, or social position. Many were amused, many were

offended. One of his poems had finally stung a leading critic so
badly that François-Marie was advised to leave town until
things had cooled off.[9]

The young poet became the guest at Fontainebleau of one of
the last and most illustrious representatives of the Old Regime,
Monsieur de Caumartin, Marquis de St. Ange, whose head was a
living history book. For days the old man entertained his guest
with tales of the age of Louis XIV. He also spoke enthusiastically
of an earlier French king, Henry IV, who had once unified France
after an agonizing civil war between Protestant and Catholic
factions. Without knowing it, the old Marquis was planting seeds
in the mind of his listener that would eventually bear fruit in
two of the most important books, *The Henriade* and *The Age of
Louis XIV*.

Before long, however, the poet was back in his favorite milieu,
Paris. He loved the glitter of high society, the attention his poetry
attracted everywhere, and the always present opportunities for
self-advancement. He certainly had no intention of spending his
life merely writing light poetry. He was to fulfill a great poetical
destiny, he believed. He had already begun to write a poetical
tragedy entitled *Oedipus* which he hoped would be as great as
anything Sophocles or Corneille had written on the theme. No
small ambition suited François-Marie. But he had not been back
in Paris long before another scandal erupted. This time he was
accused of having written a poem in which the Regent himself
was depicted as having incestuous relations with his own daughter. Society was ready to believe the worst about the man and
that the poet was quite capable of such a libel. The usually
tolerant Duke of Orleans was burned badly enough to require
that the audacious young poet exile himself from Paris. He may
have been innocent, but then the sentence could have been
severer.

As usual, François-Marie turned what could have been a
calamity into an opportunity. He became the guest of the Duke of
Sully, an old acquaintance from the Society of the Temple, at the
Duke's beautiful estate on the Loire River. From this base he
could make the rounds of other elegant country manors where
the rich and titled welcomed his witty company and encouraged
him as a raconteur and satirist. But after a few months Paris was
beckoning him back like an irresistible courtesan. He appealed to
the Regent's "sense of justice" to lift the ban on his return. This

was granted in the fall of 1716 and he joyfully returned to his old haunts and habits.

Within less than a year he was in hot water again. Another scurrilous poem against the Regent—the notorious one entitled *"J'ai vu"* ("I have seen")—was attributed to him, although this time he really was innocent. He was seized by the police and thrown into the Bastille. Like a cat who when dropped always lands on its four feet, François-Marie did not lose his balance. Free of outside distractions and allowed to live quite comfortably in the reasonably open prison, he worked furiously to finish his *Oedipus* and also found time to write the first draft of the epic poem which would eventually become the famous *The Henriade*.

When he came out of the gloomy old fortress in April, 1718, he not only had some new works in hand, he also bore a brand-new name. He no longer called himself François-Marie Arouet but Arouet de Voltaire or, soon, simply Voltaire. Why he chose this name has been the subject of a long and popular scholarly debate.[10] In any case, Arouet would soon be forgotten; Voltaire, never.

In November, 1718, Voltaire's *Oedipus* opened in Paris at the Comédie Française. This was a Greek tragedy in neoclassical dress with a love interest. The twenty-four-year-old playwright had mixed his ingredients just right to make a combination irresistible to the audience of the time. *Oedipus* was an instant success. The plot about a man who had fulfilled his fate by killing his father and marrying his mother was one which, as Aristotle had long before pointed out, was sure to make people shudder with fear and respond with pity. The horrible situation compounded of patricide and incest was sweetened somewhat by the addition of a devoted lover for Queen Jocasta, a role which Voltaire had written into the play only at the insistence of the actors, who knew that this was needed to make the drama palatable to Parisian audiences. The form of the play was easily comprehensible with its unities of time, place, and action, and the alexandrine verses in which the dialogue and choruses were presented sounded pleasant to the ear. Also, and perhaps most important, the acting was excellent.

But there was another element that made the play even more appealing to its first audience. It was shocking not only in its plot; its dialogue was at several points positively scandalous. Gods were spoken of with obvious irreverence. Oracles and priests were held up to ridicule. Voltaire's Queen Jocasta delivered lines such as: "These priests are not what the vile rabble think them; their knowledge springs from our credulity." [11] The spirit of defiance of authority, divine and earthly, radiated through the words of the sceptical and liberal young playwright. Audiences were scandalized and delighted. The play broke all performance records of the day. The playwright became at once famous. A handsome profit awaited him at the box office.

Would success spoil Voltaire? Not at all; it would simply inspire him to try to scale new heights of creative aspiration by producing new works to dazzle the imagination of his public. Within little more than a year he had another Greek-style tragedy ready for performance. It was called *Artemire*. It was a failure. But Voltaire could take failure as well as he took success. Instead of being unduly discouraged, he turned his attention back to the epic poem he had been writing off and on. "The most precious thing in the world" he called this verse saga of the struggles and successes of King Henry IV.[12] Throughout his life Henry would remain his favorite hero—lovable, tolerant Henry who had healed the French nation's wounds after years of grueling religious conflict. Henry, enemy of superstition and fanaticism, friend of culture, embodied the wisdom, courage, and humor so much needed, Voltaire believed, to bring France to greatness again in his new and troubled century. But the intolerant French authorities were in no mood to listen to a work that extolled the virtues of a man, even of a king, who had initiated a policy of religious tolerance which had later been reversed by one of his successors, Louis XIV. Its author must be subversive to have conceived of such a work as a fitting subject for a national French epic. No permit for publication was forthcoming. The authorities underestimated the determination and ingenuity of Voltaire. He managed to get his epic, then called *The League*, later retitled *The Henriade*, clandestinely printed in 1723 at Rouen. Copies were smuggled into Paris where they were eagerly circulated. France at last had the epic poem for which it had waited so long.

Voltaire's *Oedipus* and *The League* were the twin peaks of his accomplishment during this period of his life. He could well feel exhilarated to be celebrated both as a great tragedian and a great epic poet before he was thirty. And with success and celebrity came new rewards. Beautiful women willingly shared his bed.

Wealthy and titled hosts vied to entertain him. Even the doors of royalty swung open before him, and the new French king and queen applauded his plays and granted him an annuity. He became known abroad, and foreign men of letters wrote to congratulate and advise him. The king of England sent him a gold watch. New works flowed from his pen: a new tragedy, *Mariamne;* a one-act comedy, *The Indiscreet One;* a declaration of faithlessness or rather a declaration of a new natural religion to replace orthodox faith, the notorious *Epistle to Urania.* New opportunities to make money presented themselves, and Voltaire always took advantage of them.

There were some dissonant notes in this symphony of success. Voltaire's father died (1722). He himself nearly died of smallpox (1723). But nothing seemed capable of depressing for long Voltaire's indefatigable creative spirit. He was seemingly at the height of his powers and ready to astonish the world with new accomplishments.

Then, suddenly, all of this changed. In the fall of 1725 he had a violent quarrel with an obscure nobleman, the Chevalier de Rohan-Chabot, who had been needling him about his name. Later Rohan-Chabot had sent hirelings to lure Voltaire into a trap and thrash him. The poet's outrage over the attack was later increased by the failure of his noble friends to come to his defense, or even to give him sympathy. Incensed, he challenged the Chevalier to a duel, which was contemptuously declined. Swaggering around Paris armed with pistols, Voltaire was finally arrested in April, 1726, at the instigation of the Rohan-Chabot family and thrown into the Bastille.

This time his stay in the prison was to be quite brief. He wrote a letter to the proper authorities offering to leave France for England in exchange for his release. Glad to get rid of the troublemaker, the police let him out on May 3, 1726. As soon as he could make arrangements, Voltaire left Paris for the port of Calais. From there he sailed across the channel to begin a self-imposed exile in England.

IV   *English Interlude (1726–1729)*

It was in the midst of spring that I disembarked near London. The sky was cloudless, as in the loveliest days of Southern France; the air was cooled by a gentle west wind, which increased the serenity of

nature and inclined men's minds to joy . . . I landed near Greenwich,
on the banks of the Thames. This beautiful river, which never over-
flows, and whose banks are adorned with greenery all year long, was
covered for the space of six miles with two rows of merchant-vessels.
Their sails were all spread in honor of the King and Queen, who were
cruising on the river in a gilded barge, preceded by boats full of
musicians, and followed by a thousand little rowing-boats. Each of
these had two oarsmen, and all the rowers were dressed as our pages
were in olden times, with long hose and little jackets decorated with
a large silver badge on the shoulder. Everyone of these watermen
showed by his looks, his dress, and his plumpness that he lived in
freedom and in a land of plenty.[13]

What a sense of excitement Voltaire must have felt to be in a
country where he could breathe freely the air of liberty. What a
relief to put behind him the injustices and restraints of France!
He had come to England to recollect himself, to learn, and, as
always, to work. He lost no time in getting started on his new
and constantly challenging venture. As he had already become
acquainted with an influential Englishman in France, the exiled
Henry Saint-John, Viscount Bolingbroke, he had some letters of
recommendation to Englishmen who would be of use to him. His
reputation as a dramatist and poet had preceded him, and he was
soon received into the best social circles in London, even into the
royal court itself. His first task was to get settled and to learn the
English language. An English merchant, Everard Fawkener,
befriended him. Voltaire went to live at Fawkener's estate in
Wandsworth where he could pursue his studies and writings
comfortably and without distraction. Much of the time, however,
he was busily exploring his new environment and getting acquainted with every aspect of it. He was determined to satisfy
his curiosity about the English. He would, as usual, "go straight
to the facts."

The facts, Voltaire soon discovered, were very complicated. To
gather and interpret them he had to be constantly on the alert
not to miss anything essential to understanding the enigma that
was the English character and culture. He read English philosophy—especially the works of John Locke—and talked with
English philosophers such as Samuel Clarke and George Berke-
ley. He did his best to fathom the theories of English scientists,
centering his attention on Sir Isaac Newton's theory of gravita-
tion. He immersed himself in English literature, met the chief

living English authors including Jonathan Swift and Alexander Pope, and saw performances of plays by William Shakespeare, Joseph Addison, William Congreve, and John Gay. The variety of English religious sects especially fascinated him. Soon he was sorting out the differences among the Anglicans, Presbyterians, Socinians (Unitarians), and Quakers, noting the diversity of their religious beliefs and practices with precision and wit. As a good bourgeois he immediately grasped the significance of the London Stock Exchange. As an experienced courtier he soon had a grasp of English court intrigues, and even was suspected of entering into them. The mainspring of the whole complicated social mechanism was, he recognized, the political system, parliamentary government. That was what ensured the freedom of thought and action without which England would not be England.

As he rapidly became acquainted with the multiple facets of English culture he felt confident that he was beginning to understand not only what was right about it but also what was wrong with his own country. In a letter to his friend Thieriot urging him to pay a visit to England, he wrote in English:

You will see a nation fond of their liberty, learned, witty, despising life and death, a nation of philosophers; not but there are some fools in England, every country has its mad men; it may be French folly is pleasanter than English madness, but by God English wisdom and English honesty is above yours.[14]

He would give his full impressions to Thieriot and to the French nation in his later *Philosophical Letters,* which he would complete after his return to France. On the whole, these impressions were highly favorable even though he also found much to criticize. The weather was abominable, the food tasteless, the people often frigid. The whole British nation, he later observed, was like a barrel of British beer, "the top of which is froth, the bottom dregs, the middle excellent." [15] It was a great free nation but its cultural life could not compare with the brilliance, variety, and elegance of that of France. Frenchmen might not be free, but they were highly cultured.

During his two and a half years in England Voltaire not only observed, absorbed, and compared; he also worked as hard as ever. Amidst great acclaim his epic poem *The Henriade* was published in a deluxe English edition. This had been presaged by two

essays written in English, one on the history of the French civil
wars and the other on epic poetry. A new tragedy, *Brutus*, had
been partly drafted (in English). Materials for a new kind of
history, accurate in detail yet infused with imagination, had been
gathered. The subject was Charles XII of Sweden. How Voltaire
managed to accomplish so much in such a relatively short time
is astonishing. As Archibald Ballantyne, an English commentator
on this period of his life noted, Voltaire "always managed to get
more out of the twenty-four hours than any other two men could
do." [16]

Although his life in England had been happy, rewarding, and
productive he was always homesick for Paris, and finally in 1729
he slipped back there. England had aerated his ideas. For that he
would always be grateful. Even as an old man, he said that he
retained "something of the English in me." Not long before his
death he confided to an English visitor:

If ever I smell of a Resurrection, or come a second time on Earth, I
will pray God to make me born in England, the Land of Liberty.
There are four things which I adore that the English boast of—
Liberty, Property, Newton, and Locke.[17]

V   *The Middle Span (1729–1749)*

Five years had passed since Voltaire's return from England,
and he was again in trouble with the police over his writings.
This time the furor had come with the publication in 1734 of the
French edition of his *Philosophical Letters*, which had appeared
in England the year before. When he heard the bad news that he
was about to be arrested because authorities found the work to
be highly subversive, he was attending the wedding of his good
friend the Duke de Richelieu in Burgundy. His companion and
new mistress, Madame Emilie du Châtelet, offered to flee with
him to her country estate, Cirey, in northern Champagne. There
he would probably be quite safe, but, in case of pursuit, he
would be close enough to the border of the Duchy of Lorraine,
to slip quickly across. Voltaire gladly accepted her offer as he
did not dare go back to Paris. The police had arrested his publisher and thrown him into the Bastille; his *Philosophical Letters*
had been publicly burned; and a *lettre de cachet* had been issued

for his arrest. Besides, he and Madame du Châtelet were madly in love, and wanted to be alone.

The intervening years had been among the most successful in his life. By shrewd and timely investments he had added to his steadily growing fortune. Several of his new plays had been produced, one of which, *Zaïre* (1732), was a tremendous success. His *History of Charles XII* had received wide acclaim upon its publication in 1731, and promised to revolutionize the writing of history. As usual, some of his successes had stirred strong and continuing controversy. The publication of his *Epistle to Urania* (1733) brought accusations of atheism. His *Temple of Taste* drew howls of indignation from the critics who were offended by his judgment of their idols. When his former mistress and friend, the actress Adrienne Lecouvreur, died in 1730 and was not allowed a decent burial by French authorities on account of her profession, he wrote a poem in which he condemned the barbaric French attitude toward its artists by comparing it with that of the enlightened English. This had given his enemies more evidence to use against him, as did even his dedication of his hit *Zaïre* to a commoner Englishman, his fellow-bourgeois friend Everard Fawkener. He was already being called "unpatriotic," "heretical," "atheistic," "Anglophile," and "subversive" when in 1734 the *Philosophical Letters* appeared on the scene as though to confirm the worst suspicions against him. He was lucky not to have been in Paris at the time, otherwise he would have been serving time in prison rather than sipping wine with his mistress at a chateau in remote Champagne.

During the next fifteen years Voltaire's life centered on his "divine Emilie" and their "little temple dedicated to Friendship" called Cirey.[18] With Emilie at Cirey he found for the first time in his life the kind of secure and lasting love that brought him continuing happiness—at least for many years. Emilie was not only a passionate and gratifying lover; she was also a brilliant, charming, and satisfying companion. Although she was a married woman with three children and more than ten years younger than Voltaire when they fell in love, she let nothing stand in the way of their romance and life together. It is a tribute to her attractiveness, intelligence, and ingenuity that she was able to keep Voltaire happily occupied for such a long period of time so far away from his beloved Paris. Cirey, then, first of all to Voltaire

meant love. Seeing the happy lovers together there, a visitor later
wrote: "If one wanted to paint a delicious retreat, a peaceful
refuge, a calm communion of souls, amenities, talents, reciprocity
of admiration, the attraction of philosophy allied to the charm of
poetry, one would paint Cirey." [19]

As this observation also suggests, Cirey, along with love, also
meant dedication to another purpose, the pursuit of knowledge,
of "philosophy allied with poetry." And to this we must add, "the
pursuit of philosophy allied with science and history." For Voltaire and Madame du Châtelet embarked on one of the most intense and prolonged "thought-experiments" ever undertaken by
two amateurs.[20] Following in the spirit of Francis Bacon they
were taking all knowledge as their sphere. They wanted to get a
grasp on the wholeness of things so that they could become enlightened and perhaps some day be instruments of enlightenment
to others.

Madame du Châtelet was certainly an able co-worker, well
grounded in languages, mathematics, physics, and metaphysics.[21]
She shared Voltaire's great love of theater, poetry, and music. As
Voltaire put it succinctly, "Madame du Châtelet possesses all the
virtues of a great man with the graces of her sex." [22] A strange
mixture of Aspasia and Aphrodite—this was Voltaire's companion
in scholarship at Cirey. A lover of Leibniz's philosophy, Emilie
stimulated Voltaire to study metaphysics. Under her guidance, he
also probed deeper into the scientific works of Sir Isaac Newton.
In addition, together they made a thorough study of the Bible,
not for religious purposes but in order to criticize those who took
it literally to be the word of God. Voltaire, in turn, contributed
to Emilie's mental growth by encouraging her to read history,
even if he had to write a new kind of history that she would be
willing and interested to read. But it was Emilie, not Voltaire,
who seems to have been the guiding light in this unusual and
extended quest for knowledge. As Voltaire's recent biographer
A. Owen Aldridge points out, "Emilie's greatest contribution to
Voltaire's career was her example." [23] Because of that example,
Voltaire was to be quite a different kind of thinker after Cirey
than he was before he met and fell in love with Emilie, his "Lady
Newton."

The kind of mental cultivation in which Voltaire and Madame
du Châtelet were so deeply involved at Cirey did not lead to

immediate results, to numerous publications, for example, as much as it did to long-range growth. In a study of this period, Professor Ira Wade has shown how, throughout, gradually Voltaire was being transformed from a poet into a philosopher.[24] In the process he had to undergo a "total reeducation." If Emilie was not the cause of this astonishing process, which was to have such far-reaching effects on Voltaire as well as his times, she was certainly its catalyst.

Although Voltaire's Cirey period was notable more for its internal events than for its external results, it was not without significant works. This was the time in which three of his best plays —*Alzire* (1736), *Mohammed* (1742), and *Mérope* (1743)—moved French audiences to shed torrents of tears. His *Treatise on Metaphysics* was written during this time, but unlike his *Elements of the Philosophy of Newton* (1738) was not published. Some portions of his historical works, *The Age of Louis XIV* and the *Essay on Customs,* were released before they took their place in the later complete versions published in the early 1750s. New poems also appeared, the most important of which were *The Man of the World* (1736) and the *Discourses in Verse of Man* (1738). At least one of the most inflammatory anti-biblical works, *The Sermon of the Fifty,* was released around 1746. Other such works, though written during the Cirey period, would only appear much later. Finally, toward the end of this period of Voltaire's life he began to write the delightful philosophical tales that were to become, to a later age, his hallmark. *Micromégas, Memnon,* and *Zadig* were born between 1739 and 1749, and more were soon to follow. It is obvious, then, that Voltaire's and Emilie's relationship was mutually fructifying.

Although scholars usually refer to this portion of Voltaire's life as the Cirey period, as Professor Wade points out, its real unity of focus came from Madame du Châtelet rather than from Cirey, as the couple moved away from Cirey toward the end of this period.[25] Certainly neither was content to be a recluse; both loved the pleasures of high society; both liked to travel; and both liked variety in companionship and landscape. Also, Voltaire was ambitious for recognition at court and among his peers. The long periods of intense scholarly activities were lightened by trips abroad—to Holland, for example—to Paris, and to nearby Lunéville where Louis XV's father-in-law, the deposed Polish king

Stanislas Leszczinski, had established a bright and lively court. Emilie not only helped her lover with his study of science; she also backed his efforts to get a court appointment, which he received in 1745. Monsieur Arouet de Voltaire first became Royal Historiographer and later Ordinary Gentleman of the King's Bedchamber. Now he and Emilie could move freely through the glittering world of Versailles, enjoying the distractions of courtly intrigues and participating in the fêtes and spectacles. In 1746 came the realization of one of Voltaire's greatest and long-lasting ambitions, the election to the French Academy. At last he had been recognized, thanks mainly to his behind-the-scenes machinations, as a member of the "body of immortals," a living exemplar of Classicism.

From abroad a new character entered the lively and complicated drama that was Voltaire's life during this time. The young prince, Frederick of Prussia, wrote to tell Voltaire that he idolized him, and begged him to be his literary critic and philosophical guide. Eagerly the *philosophe* accepted this unexpected honor and opportunity. A lively and impassioned correspondence began which would lead soon to meetings between the two admirers and eventually to Voltaire's changing his place of residence to the royal court in Berlin. Madame du Châtelet from the start opposed the relationship. She jealously guarded her lover, and wanted no competition for his attentions.

As the years passed, however, the passionate love that had bound Voltaire to his "divine mistress" was transformed into something else, devoted friendship. Perhaps his always-precarious physical condition made it impossible for him to satisfy her always demanding physical lusts. Perhaps they had both just grown tired of each other as lovers. In any case, while they never seemed to question the importance of their intellectual and emotional bonds, they turned elsewhere for physically-based ecstasy. In his clandestine manner, Voltaire found a willing sexual partner in his recently widowed niece, Madame Denis, to whom he wrote passionate love letters which only came to light in our century. Here is a typical passage:

I am incapable of digesting, but I am capable of love. I love you; I will love you until the day I die. I embrace you a thousand times, my dear virtuosa . . . I will come for you and if the wretched state of my health permits I will throw myself at your knees and will kiss all your beauties.[26]

Emilie was open about her new lover. At a visit to King Stanislas's court at Lunéville she had fallen madly in love with a young poet and army officer, the Marquis de Saint-Lambert. When Voltaire first discovered them together he was inflamed with jealousy; later, when he had time to think it over and discuss it with Emilie, he accepted the relationship, just as once Emilie's husband had accepted Voltaire's relationship to her. But instead of the establishment of a *menage à trois* the new relationship brought disaster. At the age of forty-three Emilie became pregnant by her twenty-seven-year-old lover. Although Voltaire nursed her tenderly during her confinement and quipped that they would put the baby among her "miscellaneous works," Emilie did not survive the ordeal. Her scholarly investigations were terminated by her giving birth to a child which precipitated her death shortly afterwards. For a while, Voltaire was inconsolable. "I have lost one who was my friend for twenty-five years," he wrote Frederick, "a great man, whose only defect was being a woman." [27] And to his friend d'Argental, to whom he turned for consolation, he emoted, "I have not lost a mistress, I have lost half of myself; a soul for whom mine was made." [28]

The Cirey or Madame du Châtelet period of Voltaire's life was over. Emilie's death in 1749 released a philosopher from a cocoon that once had contained a slumbering poet.

VI *Life with Frederick (1750–1753)*

With the death of his beloved Emilie, Voltaire no longer had a "divine mistress," but there was someone waiting eagerly to become his "royal master." Prince Frederick of Prussia was now King Frederick, and he was determined to persuade France's greatest poet to illuminate the court which he had recently established at Potsdam. What Frederick wanted, he usually got. Voltaire was now available—for a price. The Prussian king could offer money, honors, and freedom, all of which appealed to the French *philosophe*. By mid-summer of 1750 Voltaire had transplanted himself from Paris to Potsdam with intentions, perhaps, of settling there permanently, assuming he could persuade his

niece Madame Denis to join him there. He had gone to prepare
a place for her.

At first all seemed well in paradise. Frederick was apparently a
budding philosopher-king who only wanted intellectual stimula-
tion and literary guidance from his distinguished guest. The royal
court certainly was no Versailles, but it was very French in its
atmosphere and aspirations. Frederick had already stocked it with
a group of lively Frenchmen, including the scientist and explorer
Pierre-Louis Moreau de Maupertuis, who had been made President of the Berlin Academy of Sciences, and the physician and
writer Julien Offroy de La Mettrie, who was a sort of atheist-in-
residence and unofficial court jester. For a while Voltaire was
flattered to be the star of Frederick's intimate dinners at which
his wit sparkled as freely as he wished; no subject was forbidden,
and a spirit of irreverent camaraderie prevailed. Frederick, for
his part, was at first quite elated over the prize which he had
successfully snared for his miniature Versailles. As Thomas
Carlyle put it, Frederick was "eager in all ways to content him,
make him happy; and keep him here, as the Talking Bird, the
Singing Tree and the Golden Water, of intelligent mankind; the
glory of one's own Court, and the envy of the world." [29]

Soon, however, the illusions all around were shattered. Frederick heard that Voltaire found his assigned duty of correcting
the king's French verse more than a little tedious. Had the
Frenchman indeed had the audacity to exclaim: "Will he never
get tired of sending me his dirty linen to wash?" [30] And Voltaire
was furious to hear that the king had once remarked of him: "I'll
need him another year at most; you squeeze the orange and then
you throw away the peel." [31] Despite the flattering reassurances
that were usually forthcoming, it soon became evident that the
two supreme egotists were becoming increasingly distrustful of
each other. "Frederick," Voltaire confided in a letter to his niece,
"still sometimes scratches with one hand, while he caresses with
the other." [32]

To make matters worse, Voltaire, as always, got involved in
complications. He meddled in Frederick's diplomatic relations.
He intrigued to help a foreign countess with whom he was probably carrying on an affair. An illegal financial deal with a Berlin
Jew ended up in lawsuits and recriminations. As a final blow to
the king's confidence in his guest's integrity, there was the widely
publicized quarrel between Voltaire and Maupertuis, which gave

birth to Voltaire's devastating *Diatribe of Doctor Akakia,* which was directed against the scientist and Frederick's academicians. Although he had laughed until he cried when Voltaire first read it to him privately, the king had strictly forbidden its publication. When afterwards Voltaire released the work to the press anyway, Frederick was enraged. He had all copies of it seized and burned. Now he considered his former mentor to be a "wicked madman," good to read but loathsome to know.

In December, 1752, Voltaire wrote his niece that he felt that "the orange had been squeezed" and that he would try to save the skin.

My only plan is to desert honorably, to take care of my health, to see you again, and forget this three years' nightmare . . . I am going to make, for my instruction, a little Dictionary for the use of kings. "My friend" means "my slave." "My dear friend" means "you are absolutely nothing to me." By "I will make you happy" understand "I will put up with you as long as I need you." "Dine with me tonight" means "I shall make fun of you this evening." The dictionary might be long; what an article for the Encyclopedia![33]

Finally, in the middle of March, 1753, Voltaire received Frederick's permission to leave Prussia. Both tried to smooth things over for the sake of appearances. But after Voltaire's departure Frederick discovered that he had taken with him a book of poems written by the king which, if published, could embarrass him greatly. (The royal poet had satirized some of his royal European peers in his poetry.) He sent orders to his representative in Frankfurt to intercept Voltaire en route and to recover from him the book of poems. This was done in such a high-handed and rough fashion that Voltaire and his niece, who had meanwhile joined him, were outraged. Soon all of Europe knew of the quarrel between the king and the philosopher.

Although this period of Voltaire's life ended, then, in discomfort and disillusionment, it was nonetheless a time of significant literary achievement and psychological growth. While he was living in Prussia he had the leisure and freedom to do the enormous amount of research required for completing his most important historical work, *The Age of Louis XIV.* This had been published in Berlin at Frederick's expense in 1751. A major philosophical tale *Micromégas* and the important philosophical

Poem on Natural Law were also written during this time. And, of course, it did inspire the production of what remains one of Voltaire's liveliest satires, *The Diatribe of Doctor Akakia*. But what Voltaire learned from the years with Frederick was probably of equal importance to what he wrote during this period. For one thing, he had learned that "when a king becomes an author, you may be sure that truth will move far from the throne." [34] Perhaps, after all, it was far better to be a philosopher dissatisfied than a courtier satisfied. He also now realized that "it is worth more to have one hundred francs in a free country than one thousand in a despotic country." [35] Even the most enlightened despot is nonetheless a despot.

VII   *Putting down Roots: "Les Délices" and Ferney (1753–1778)*

After recovering from the fiasco of Potsdam Voltaire decided to settle in Switzerland where he hoped to find a haven safe from despots, censors, and priests. The French-speaking Protestant republic of Geneva seemed to have everything he was seeking. Soon he was happily established there on a beautiful estate overlooking "the thinking man's lake" and the River Rhône, with a fine view of the mountains in the distance. "Les Délices" ("The Delights") he called the estate. With his beloved niece at his side he seemed to have found at last the essentials of the best kind of life.

Happy is he who lives in his own home with his nieces, his books, his gardens, his vineyards, his horses, his cows, his eagle, his fox and his rabbits, which rub their noses with their paws. I have all that as well as the Alps which create an admirable effect. I much prefer scolding my gardeners than paying homage to kings.[36]

His life, as usual, was full of activity. He entertained lavishly, cultivated new and influential acquaintances in the community, and dabbled in Genevan politics. Despite the town's puritanical attitudes and hostility to hedonism, he invited some of its citizens to the private theatrical performances on his estate. The renowned but exiled Genevan citizen Jean-Jacques Rousseau elicited his interest for a while by sending him high compliments along with his latest books to comment upon. Eventually the volatile Genevan was to become one of Voltaire's most despised enemies, but at first he received only admiration, understanding, and subtle teasing from his idol. As a response to receiving a copy of Rousseau's famous *Discourse on Inequality* in 1755, Voltaire penned his delightful letter that begins "I have received, Sir, your new book against the human race, and I thank you for it." [37]

Never a recluse, Voltaire retained an intense interest in what was happening in the world outside Geneva. The Lisbon earthquake of 1755 precipitated in him the profoundest anguish which found expression in his famous *Poem on the Lisbon Earthquake.* He kept up a voluminous correspondence with friends and acquaintances throughout Europe. He began to write articles for the French *Encyclopedia,* that great forum of enlightened ideas which Denis Diderot and Jean le Rond D'Alembert were developing in Paris, under the very noses of those whom it would eventually help to destroy. In fact, it was an article on Geneva in the *Encyclopedia* which caused trouble between Voltaire and the Genevan city fathers. Written by D'Alembert but with the approval and perhaps even collaboration of Voltaire, the article deplored the absence of a theater in Geneva but praised the pastors of the city for their "socinianism" (a religious point-of-view supposedly similar to deism). The lighthearted seigneur of "Les Delices" was soon made to feel very uncomfortable in the former theocracy of Calvin.

To move or not to move? That was the question. Voltaire decided to move. But not far. Just across the border into French territory. The chateau of Ferney was his next and last place of residence.

Settled in at Ferney, Voltaire was able at last to put down roots and send out new branches. He was now free and able to do pretty much as he pleased. His refuge was secure, with easy escape routes if they should ever be needed, poised as it was on the border of two countries. His vast wealth made it possible for him to be a "grand seigneur" of his small domain, capable of bestowing benefits wherever he thought they were needed and deserved.[38] Madame Denis was his constant companion, able and willing to meet his emotional and sexual needs. His fame was ever growing and the power of his pen undiminished. He was now certainly in a position to do whatever he wanted, and what he wanted was "to do a little good."

In the years that followed his move to Ferney he gradually

transformed a little settlement of fifty people into a flourishing
community of over twelve hundred inhabitants. Vineyards were
restored, roads improved, industries established, housing built,
and workers given profitable and fair employment. Ferney became known for its fine watches and silk stockings. There serfdom
had been abolished, and men were free from exploitation. Voltaire was in his heaven, and all was right with the world. He
even built a little church on his estate, inscribing over its portals
"Deo erexit Voltaire." (To God erected by Voltaire.) "Two great
names!", commented an enraptured visitor.

The chateau at Ferney became a place of hermitage, so much
so that Voltaire dubbed himself "the innkeeper of Europe." Various and sundry persons streamed there to pay homage to the
always entertaining *philosophe.* One of his young French visitors
wrote this glowing account of the "Patriarch of Ferney":

He is the king and the father of the country where he lives; he provides the happiness of everything around him, and he is as good a
father as he is a poet. If he were cut into two and I were to see on
one side the man I have read and on the other the one whom I
encounter, I would not know toward which I would be drawn . . . He
will always be the best edition of his books." [39]

His managerial activities and his social life were only two
facets of his many-faceted existence at Ferney. From morning to
night he worked tirelessly, often in bed, dictating to his secretary.
New plays and poems were composed. Letters went out daily to
all parts of Europe. A major new work, the *Philosophical Dictionary* (1764), was prepared as a one-man guide to enlightenment and a rival to the mammoth *Encyclopedia.* Innumerable
dialogues, pamphlets, satires, articles, and other pieces, usually
grouped together under the name *facéties,* flowed from his pen.
The philosophical tales, which would assure him lasting fame,
continued to appear periodically, including the most famous of
all, *Candide* (1759). It is astonishing that one man could have
written so much. "About fifteen million of Voltaire's written
words have come down to us," estimates Theodore Besterman,
"enough to make twenty *Bibles.*" [40] And a large portion of these
words were written during the final Ferney period of the author's
life.

This was also the time during which Voltaire underwent his last and most striking transformation. The man of letters became a man of action. Wielding his pen as a sword, he launched a campaign against the forces of superstition and intolerance, a campaign which would continue until his death. He would do everything in his power to "crush the infamy" of religious fanaticism. He furiously lashed out against the authorities who in 1765 had arrested and executed a young man, La Barre, for supposedly impious behavior. (The young man's "crime" had been partially "confirmed" by his possession of Voltaire's *Philosophical Dictionary*.) "I am still a bit fervent despite my age," the old warrior wrote. "Oppressed innocence moves me; persecution makes me indignant and ferocious." [41]

The best known of all the cases of "oppressed innocence" that riveted Voltaire's attention was the Calas affair of 1762. A Protestant merchant from Toulouse, Jean Calas was accused of murdering his son to prevent his converting to Catholicism. The Calas family claimed that the youth in a depression had committed suicide. After a long trial the elder Calas was found guilty and executed. Looking into the case carefully, Voltaire became convinced that the executed man had been completely innocent and had become the victim of religious intolerance on the part of those who tried him. He waged a campaign to reverse the court's decision and clear the dead man's name. In 1764 his long and arduous efforts were crowned with success. Jean Calas was officially exonerated, and Voltaire was now known not just as a famous author, but as "the defender of Calas." After that he helped other innocent victims of religious bigotry and social injustice, becoming in the process a real-life "Don Quixote of the oppressed." The main literary monument of all of these undertakings was his *Treatise on Tolerance* (1763), a work which used the Calas case as a focal point around which to discuss the history of intolerance and the philosophy of toleration. The essence of his position has been well summed up in the aphorism attributed (although mistakenly) to him: "I disapprove of what you say, but I will defend to the death your right to say it." [42]

Thus preoccupied with his continuous efforts to defend the weak against the strong, to make his utopian experiment at Ferney village a success, to keep his beloved niece happy and his household at peace, to entertain the host of visitors, to fend off enemies, and, above all, to write, Voltaire grew old. But despite his advancing age he retained all of his wit, charm, and vibrancy. In 1775 one of his visiting young female admirers wrote a striking description of the "old man of the mountains" in his eighties:

I expected to see a decrepit face, a caricature, but I saw a physiognomy full of fire, grace, and expression. In truth, I find him charming but his tone, his politeness are even better than that . . . He put on his wig today for my sake, because I had told him that I found him very good-looking and twenty years younger than in his night-cap. In fact he has the air of a courtier of Louis XIV. He holds himself marvellously, is not round shouldered, and walks very nimbly for a man of his age. He has the most beautiful eyes in the world, still so brilliant that one can barely support their lustre. And with it all he has an air of goodness.[43]

VIII   *Going Back Home: Paris, 1778*

Voltaire was now, more than ever before, a national hero. Funds were raised to erect a statue to him in the capital. His new play, *Irène,* was soon to open at the Comédie française. Paris was calling its most illustrious citizen to come home. The old Parisian must have been filled with nostalgia for the old familiar faces, favorite haunts, and unique sights which he had not seen for almost thirty years. Louis XV had died in 1776 and a new king, Louis XVI, was on the throne. Perhaps he would look more favorably on Voltaire than did his grandfather. The new queen, Marie Antoinette, had reportedly wept at one of Voltaire's plays and had expressed a desire to "embrace" him. And the always restless and selfish Madame Denis urged her frail uncle to take her back to the center of French social life. Finally, the temptation to return in triumph to Paris was irresistible. On February 8, 1778, Voltaire left Ferney for a visit to the French capital. He was never to return.

The French people received him with adulation. Their champion and protector, their hope for the future, was at long last in their midst. Government authorities dared not harm him, although royalty did not condescend to receive him. Unending streams of visitors came to see the eighty-three-year-old *philo-*

sophe day and night. Though he was now little more than skin and bones, his energy seemed undiminished. His old friends marveled that his mind and memory had lost so little of their power. Those piercing eyes still sparkled in the thin, skull-like face. His expression was, as always, ironic.

The past as well as the future paid tribute to him. The English ambassador came, awakening in his memory those long-past happy years abroad. The American, Benjamin Franklin, came, bringing his grandson to be blessed by the old deist. Voltaire laid his hand on the boy's head and pronounced in English the words: "God and liberty." [44]

Doctors forbade him to attend the opening night performance of *Irène*, but he did put in an appearance several nights later. The actors and audience exulted in his presence. While he was still seated in his box an actor came to place a crown of laurels on his head. At the end of the play, amidst tumultous applause, his bust was crowned on stage. Voltaire was hailed as hero, genius, and savior of humanity.

But all the excitement and worship was too much for the old man. He overextended his stay in the captivating city and over-taxed his now quite limited strength. Now there was an unwanted caller knocking at his door—Death.

Previously he had written:

I am not afraid of death which is rapidly drawing near . . . but I have an unconquerable aversion for the way in which one dies in our holy religion, catholic, apostolic and Roman. It seems to me extremely ridiculous to have oneself annointed with oil to go into the next world as one has the axle of one's carriage greased on a trip.[45]

Still the same old Voltaire, joking on the brink of the grave.

He lingered on through the spring, as though reluctant to bid Paris adieu. Despite his agony, he rallied when they brought news that one of his final efforts to clear an innocent man's name had been successful. The King's Council had reversed its judgment against Lally, the former governor of India, who had been unjustly condemned and executed fifteen years earlier. The old *philosophe* managed to dictate one last letter. To the vindicated man's son he wrote:

The dying man revives upon learning this great news; he embraces
M. de Lally fondly; he sees that the king is the defender of justice;
he will die content.[46]

In order to ensure a decent burial for himself and perhaps,
also, to protect the rights of his heirs, he had signed a confession
of faith shortly before his death, stating simply that he was dying
as a Catholic and hoped for divine pardon if he had ever offended
the Church. But to his secretary Wagnière he had entrusted another confession which represented his real and deepest conviction. This one read: "I die adoring God, loving my friends, not
hating my enemies and detesting superstition." [47]
He died around eleven o'clock at night on May 30, 1778.
Even his death, however, precipitated the usual Voltairian
complications. Not satisfied with the old heretic's confession, the
clergy refused him burial in holy ground. Ferney was too far
away to take the body even if authorities there should be co-
operative, which was unlikely. Voltaire's nephew, the Abbé
Mignot, took matters in hand in a way that would have amused
his uncle. He quickly had the body embalmed, placed it in a
sitting position in a carriage, clad in a dressing gown and wearing
a night cap, and smuggled it safely out of the city. Six horses
carried the corpse to the monastery of Scellières in Champagne,
which was under Mignot's jurisdiction; there it was given a quiet
and sanctified burial.[48]
But Voltaire's body was not to rest there for long. In July,
1791, it was brought back to Paris by order of the leaders of the
French Revolution. A triumphant procession, carrying portraits
of both Voltaire and his enemy, Jean-Jacques Rousseau, escorted
the remains of the "fathers of the Revolution" to the national
mausoleum of French heroes, the Pantheon. On the sarcophagus
that contained Voltaire's coffin were inscribed these words: "He
avenged Calas, La Barre, Sirven and Montbailli. Poet, philosopher, historian, he caused the human spirit to take a great leap
forward; he prepared us to be free." [49]

CHAPTER 2

Man of Sensibility: Voltaire as Poet

I "Great Poet in an Age without Poetry"

"POETRY is the music of the soul," Voltaire wrote, "and above all of great and of feeling souls."[1] Although he himself might not have realized either in theory or practice the full implications of this definition, the very fact that he formulated it in this way is highly significant. For it suggests that Voltaire was not the cold conservative defender of neoclassical traditions which he has sometimes been made out to be. As David Williams in a study of Voltaire's literary criticism has pointed out, Voltaire was not trying to reestablish Classicism; he was trying to revive the greatness behind it."[2] And this greatness—the greatness which was, in his mind, best exemplified by Jean Racine—depended not just upon a highly developed taste and a sound rational judgment in constructing works of art but also on the inspiration of genius. Knowledge, talent, and common sense might be enough to make a superior versifier, but to these must be added an uncommon sensibility in order to make a true poet. The French poet and literary critic Nicolas Boileau showed what could be achieved by a man of genius, Voltaire believed, even when he was working within the narrow confines of French literary usage. His works, Voltaire held, were "masterpieces of reasoning as well as poetry" in which true and useful ideas were communicated in an always pleasing manner.[3] But even superior to Boileau was the tragic poet Racine whom Voltaire praised frequently for his "continued elegance," "purity of language," "truth of character," as well as for his "grandeur without bombast" and "fidelity to nature," all qualities which Voltaire admired greatly and tried to emulate in his own poetry.[4]

If great models, high ideals, and indefatigable efforts could

make a great poet, Voltaire certainly would have succeeded in
his lifetime undertaking to make of himself another Racine or
Virgil. He and his contemporaries were convinced that he had
succeeded in reaching his goal; today we know that they were
sadly mistaken. If Voltaire was considered great, it was only
because no one superior to him was then writing poetry, or, to
put it less kindly, his contemporaries were even worse poets than
he. He seemed a giant only because he was being compared with
pygmies. A few had the critical judgment and aesthetic taste to
recognize his lack of poetical genius—Denis Diderot said that he
was "second-rate in all the genres"—but throughout his life Voltaire and his generation retained the illusion that he was indeed
a great poet.

All the external trappings of the great poet were clearly evident. Following the neoclassical views of his time, he wrote works
which clearly exemplified the traditional grand genres of poetry.
Imitating ancient and modern models he wrote an epic poem,
The Henriade, to show that the genre was not beyond the reach
of a Frenchman. He wrote a large number of tragedies and
comedies which he was convinced were not only exemplary of
the principles of good classical taste but were the expressions of
a "feeling soul" with power to move and improve audiences. In
addition, he wrote innumerable lighter verse—satires, epistles,
contes in verse, and "fugitive pieces" which show not only the
classicist still at work but also reveal another, truer poet using
his own imagination and at times breaking free of all restraints
to find his own form of self-expression. As we shall see, it is only
this last, less well known poet that we really can care about and
respond to in our day when we search for Voltaire the poet. Not
that his other poetry is without value and interest. But it no
longer seems to be expressive of genuine emotion; it is not "the
music of the soul." It is as dead as its producer. It is the work of
a skilled versifier who has properly been characterized as "a
great poet in an age without poetry." [5]

II *Declaration of Sceptical Faith:* The Epistle to Urania *(1722)*

We can be thankful to one of Voltaire's early mistresses, Mme
de Rupelmonde, for questioning him about religion so searchingly
that the young poet was stimulated to make a confession of faith
in the form of a poetical epistle. *The Epistle to Urania* (1722) is

a defiant declaration of independence from Christian orthodoxy and a defense of natural religion.[6] Like a new Lucretius, the poet proceeds to tear off the blindfold of superstition which, to him, is Christian dogma and to offer a rational alternative to it. The God of Christians is quite different from the God he believes in and adores. To project upon this true deity the characteristics and actions attributed to God by Christianity would dishonor and insult Him. It is because Voltaire loves God that he feels he must reject Christianity.

Fortunately for the honest searcher, the poet believes, there is an alternative to religious supernaturalism. This is deism or natural religion. This religion has no enigmatic Christ figure. It attracts no pitiless fanatics and ambitious priests. It does not promote hate in the name of love. It is a positive rather than a negative religion. Communicants in its fold are judged by their virtues, not by their sacrifices. Their God is a god of justice who has no need of human attentions and is not a reflection of human follies, prejudices, and imperfections. This is the deity which is worthy of Urania's adoration; belief in such a god dispels fear of death and makes it possible to live a happier life now.

In its uncompromising scepticism, its hostility to Christianity, and its demand that religion have human relevance, Voltaire's *The Epistle to Urania* resembles *A Free Man's Worship* by Bertrand Russell, a thinker who has paid tribute to the earlier sceptic's influence. But Voltaire, unlike Russell, was no agnostic; an affirmative deism rather than stoical resignation was the faith by which he lived and died. He was more like some later radical critics of Christianity (e.g., Leo Tolstoy and Sören Kierkegaard) who, springing out of a Christian tradition which had lost its integrity, vitality, and authority, struck out, in the name of the true Christian spirit, against organized Christianity or Christendom.

III   *Aesthetic Manifesto:* The Temple of Taste *(1733)*

> The structure's of a simple taste,
> Each ornament is justly placed;
> The whole's arranged with so much care,
> Art seems to copy nature there;
> The beauteous structure fills the sight,
> Not with surprise, but with delight.[7]

This description of Voltaire's first sight of the Temple of Taste is also, according to Theodore Besterman, an excellent description of the classical style. It is one of the most important passages of a poem entitled *The Temple of Taste* (1733) which summed up the successful poet's ideas on aesthetics and literary criticism at the time it was written. Although it was intended as a support and defense of true Classicism rather than an attack on it, the work upset contemporary critics by its mixture of poetry and prose, its attack on certain highly esteemed authors, and its author's sometimes condescending and arrogant tone.

The Temple of Taste as Voltaire envisaged it was "surrounded with a crowd of virtuosos, artists, and connoisseurs of various kinds, who endeavored to enter, but did not succeed." [8] The description of those who begged admittance to the temple, their various entreaties, and the reasons given for or against their admission by Criticism, the guardian of the portal, takes up much of the content of the poem, and gives the author plenty of opportunity for witty comment and brilliant satire. All pedantic and ignorant commentators, all restorers of texts, all inept, imitative, and pretentious artists are barred from the temple. So are envious critics, "the obscure enemies of all-shining merit, those insects of society, which are taken notice of because they bite." [9] Also barred are a motley lot of writers, including a composer of a metaphysical romance, an author of a poetical miscellany, a writer of an academic speech, a presenter of a mandate cast in an affected and overrefined style. The guard Criticism was also prepared to reject musicians who had attempted to graft foreign tastes in music onto those of his native land, as "nothing can be as ridiculous as French scenes sung in the Italian taste, except Italian ones sung in the French taste." [10] And equally unwelcome to the temple's precincts were malicious slanderers of other writers as well as mere versifiers whose works, while proper, totally lacked feeling.

Who, then, would be allowed to enter into the Temple of Taste? Having gleefully settled some accounts with his enemies, Voltaire now gladly shares his enthusiasm for some of his favorite artists with his readers. He is happy to see that already received and honored in the temple are "the learned Fontenelle" (who was still living when Voltaire wrote this poem), the Roman poet and hedonist Lucretius, the German philosopher Gottfried Wilhelm Leibniz, whom Criticism had admitted, the author tells us, "because he had written tolerably good Latin verses" and in order "to soften by such an example the presence of his scientific brethren." [11]

In the glowing temple of the God of Taste, Voltaire is not surprised to find hanging works by the French painters Nicolas Poussin, Charles Le Brun, and Eustache Le Sueur. He is also not surprised to find absent from its precincts formerly popular but second-rate writers such as St. Evremond and Voiture. Only truly great artists, real geniuses, are allowed to inhabit the temple's inner sanctum. These artists—Fénelon, Bossuet, Corneille, Racine, La Fontaine, Boileau, and Molière—are the "greats" of the Age of Louis XIV, an age which to Voltaire marked the apogee of artistic achievement. Pausing here, the author points out that all of these superior geniuses had the characteristic of self-criticism, the capacity to recognize and the desire to rectify imperfections in their works. This capacity, by the way, Voltaire himself certainly possessed.

After the author's final remark that he has discovered that the God of Taste is very hard to please and that "the works which he criticizes the most are the ones he likes best," the poem ends with advice from the God of Taste on how to distinguish false from true taste.[12] Lack of grace, an affected air, and a lack of the natural fire of inspiration are sure signs of False Taste.

The Temple of Taste remains an important work to the student of Voltaire in that it is a monument to the author's taste at the time. But, as David Williams has shown in *Voltaire, Literary Critic*, in its later editions it also gives us a fascinating record of the dynamic evolutionary nature of Voltaire's literary taste.[13] That taste reflected both Voltaire's unchanging principles and the ever changing conditions within which he pursued his tasks as a critic and evaluator of literature and the other arts. Criticism was always to him not just a field for inquiry but a field of contest. As he vanquished old enemies from the field (e.g., J.-B. Rousseau) new ones appeared to take their place. The critic had always to be faithfully on guard before the Temple of Taste.

If Voltaire never hesitated to pass judgment as a critic, he did hesitate to set forth with any finality the principles by which he performed his critical functions. Raymond Naves, in *Le Goût de Voltaire (The Taste of Voltaire)*, attributes this hesitation to Voltaire's "anti-geometrical spirit," his distrust of abstract, metaphysical ideas.[14] But throughout his critical writing,

50

VOLTAIRE

Voltaire continually stressed the importance of certain formal qualities which characterized, he believed, all beautiful works of art. Unity, clarity, simplicity are paramount among these. We may not be able to define good taste with any precision, Voltaire admits, but we certainly can recognize, develop, and apply it. The best kind of taste, he believed, prefers "to imitate nature with the highest fidelity, energy, and grace." [15]

IV *Heralding* The Henriade: An Essay on Epic Poetry *(1727)*

While he was living in England and working toward getting his epic poem *The Henriade* published there, Voltaire wrote in English an essay that was intended as a theoretical justification and promotion of this work. Published in 1727 in its English edition and later in a revised edition (1732) in French, *An Essay on Epic Poetry* defines and surveys the field of epic poetry, praises and criticizes its leading practitioners, and concludes by raising the question as to why a great French national epic has not previously been written. The answer suggested was that it had taken a genius such as Voltaire to write one.

The *Essay* is remarkably well written for an author who had only known English for a short time—he undoubtedly had considerable help from his English friends in editing the work for publication—and is still worth reading as an introduction to the theory and practice of epic poetry. It attests to the fact that the ambitious young epicist has done his homework in the history of the epic, and that he has carefully constructed his forthcoming work upon the very best models, both ancient and modern. At the start he states his view that examples of an art work are far more important than rules; that poems far outweigh treatises on poetry. He then proceeds to write a weighty treatise on poetry.

First, he focuses on his target. An epic is, as he sees it, a discourse in verse relating some great action.[16] Judging by the wide variety of examples historically included within the genre, it doesn't seem to matter, he notes, whether the action is single or complex, the place single or manifold, the hero one or more, happy or unhappy, king or other, the scene on earth or in heaven or in hell.[17] Unity of action, however, does seem to be essential to all good epics, otherwise attention cannot be riveted and sustained. It is also important, he believes, to use all means available to give variety to the work. Further, as the epic's purpose is to narrate an action, the author should be sure that the action is great and awe-inspiring enough, or at least so fascinating, that the audience is delighted and satisfied with it.

Beyond these generalizations, Voltaire is wary of setting down ground rules of epic poetry. The tricks of the trade have varied as widely as the styles and languages in which epics have been written. Here Voltaire strikes a theme that will become stronger and more frequent in his later work: the relativity and volatility of taste. What will seem a sublime effect in an English epic may appear bizarre to a Frenchman and ludicrous to an Italian. What is moving in an episode to a Spaniard may be totally meaningless to an Englishman. Still, Voltaire thinks that the best way to understand epic poetry is to study its exemplifications in different countries and in different ages. In doing this, we certainly should show all due respect to the ancients—to Homer and Virgil especially—but we should also pay attention to what has been achieved in the field by the moderns. Present productions may turn out to be as deserving of our respect as past.

As he surveys the chief works of epic poetry, he at the same time passes judgment upon them. Homer's *Iliad*, he claims, lacks coherence, depicts unworthy gods and unconvincing heroes, and with its numerous battles becomes quite monotonous.[18] Much greater is Virgil's *Aeneid* which he considers the most beautiful monument of antiquity.[19] For him Virgil's works remain "the delight of all ages and the pattern of all poets." [20] The Portuguese epicist Vaz de Camoëns is to him a good example of how true genius can overcome all obstacles to create a great epic, *The Luciads*.[21] The Italian author of *Jerusalem Liberated*, Torquato Tasso, deals with a subject, the liberation of the Holy Land, that is nobler and far more awe-inspiring than Homer's *Iliad* which only dealt with the attempt to liberate a beautiful woman.[22] Despite its flaws, Milton's *Paradise Lost* is "the noblest work which human imagination has ever attempted." [23]

In raising, finally, the question of why there is no first-rate French example of the epic to edify the public, Voltaire takes the opportunity to turn a treatise on literary criticism to an ideological end. The reason does not lie in the limitations of the French language or in the "shackles of rhyme." It lies rather, he holds, in the fact that French poets "are tied down to most insupportable and insignificant rules." [24] The French language does not lack loftiness, it lacks freedom. "For it is with our heroic poetry, as

with our trade," he writes, "we come up to the English in neither,
for want of being a free nation." [25] The message here, then, is
the same as in his *Philosophical Letters*. What is needed is increased economic, literary, philosophical, and religious toleration.[26] Liberated Voltaire will give France its epic.[27]

V   *Ideal of a Tolerant Monarch:* The Henriade *(1728)*

Although *The Henriade* today has become a museum-piece
and is seldom read except by students of French literature, in its
own time it was hailed as a masterpiece greater than both the
Iliad and the *Aeneid*, and brought its author fame and fortune.
Certainly the work qualified as an epic: it related the struggles
and triumph of a great hero, Henry IV; it narrated in verse
stirring events, the French Civil wars, in which two radically
different forces, Catholic and Protestant, were pitted against
each other; and it manifested, at least on the surface, the
unity of action that Voltaire deemed essential to such a work.
The young student of epic poetry had obviously done his homework well. His tone is properly serious; his language is eloquent;
and his narration is smooth, swift, and forceful.

Like his classical predecessors, Voltaire presents his hero in a
variety of situations, including a visit to the underworld and an
interval of love-making. For the classical deities he substitutes
more believable modern personifications such as Discord, Fanaticism, and Truth. The first lines are in the proper epic tradition
showing the influence of Homer and Virgil:

> The chief renowned, who ruled in France I sing,
> By right of conquest and of birth a King;
> In various sufferings resolute and brave;
> Faction he quelled: he conquered, and forgave.[28]

These lines are soon followed by the invocation to the muses to
be expected in an epic:

> O heaven-born truth, descend, celestial muse,
> Thy power, thy brightness in my verse infuse.
> May kings attentive hear thy voice divine,
> To teach the monarchs of mankind is thine.

> 'Tis thine to war-enkindling realms to show
> What dire effects from cursed division flow.[29]

The last two lines suggest Voltaire's deeper concern in the poem
—to depict the disastrous consequences that can result from
religious bigotry and intolerance, and to contribute to the crushing of the infamy of fanaticism in all its multifarious forms. This
is especially apparent in his striking recounting in Canto II of the
massacre of Protestants by Catholics on St. Bartholomew's Day,
which, in another place, he referred to as "this execrable tragedy
[in which] one half of the nation butchered the other, with a
dagger in one hand and a crucifix in the other." [30] The moral
message of *The Henriade* is apparent here as in every canto, a
message which Voltaire tirelessly reiterated throughout his life
and works. He put it succinctly in his prose account of the life
of Henry IV:

It is a very deplorable thing that the religion which enjoins the forgiveness of injuries should have occasioned so many murders to be committed, and this only in consequence of the maxim that all who think
differently from us are in a state of reprobation, and that we are
bound to hold such in abhorrence.[31]

The relevance of Voltaire's message was certainly not missed
by those against whom it was delivered: the intolerant forces of
the church and state. The poem itself was not to be tolerated,
and its publication was not permitted. Published secretly, however, in Rouen in 1723 and soon smuggled into Paris, its success
was instantaneous. It brought new fame and notoriety to its
already controversial author, who had to search elsewhere for a
milieu in which his poem could be published and appreciated
freely. This he found in England, where *The Henriade* was
published in 1728 to the acclaim of a nation.

As Voltaire cast the materials of his epic in neoclassical form,
today *The Henriade* may be called "the masterpiece of a defunct
artistic form." [32] Yet despite its defects as poetry it is still worth
reading, if only to gain an understanding of the aesthetic and
moral commitments to which Voltaire remained true for the rest
of his life. In Henry IV he found and celebrated a hero and an
ideal of a monarchy worthy of his respect and admiration. He

described him more fully elsewhere in an historical prose account:

Had Henry IV been only the bravest, most merciful, most upright, and most honest man of his age, his kingdom must have been ruined. It required a prince who knew equally well how to make war and peace, who was acquainted with all the wounds of his kingdom, and the remedies to be applied to them; who was capable of attending to the most important and most trivial affairs, of reforming whatever was amiss, and of doing everything that could be done; all these qualifications met in Henry IV. To the policy of Charles the Wise, he added the openness of Francis I and the goodness of Louis XII.[33]

VI *Earthly Paradise:* The Man of the World *(1736)*

In a delightful poem entitled *Le Mondain* (*The Man of the World,* 1736), written a few years after *The Temple of Taste,* Voltaire gave eloquent testimony to the values of civilized life. In it he rejoices that he is living at a time when the variety of refined pleasures—of dining, looking at paintings and sculptures, listening to music, and so on—are readily available. Others may long for Eden and condemn the age as profane and decadent; for his part the poet accepts the world the way it is, and makes the most of it. Abundance, not poverty, is the mother of the arts, sciences, and inventions. Luxury is a necessity to living the best kind of life. Those who consider private enterprise such as trading to be selfish fail to take into account how such individual effort contributes to the public happiness. Even if he could, the poet would not want to return to Eden. There were no luxuries in Eden; it was a rather primitive place inhabited by two unattractive ancestors whom we would be ashamed to introduce into the polite society of today. Who would want to sleep on the bare ground when he could sleep in a comfortable bed? Or reduce love-making to mere animal instinct? In the state of nature man is a helpless, wretched creature. Without the accoutrements of civilization, we would not have the means for living at the highest level of human achievement. So who, in his right mind, would voluntarily renounce the world and withdraw from it in expectation of finding fulfillment? Let ascetics seek paradise through self-renunciation, mortification, and austerities. Voltaire himself prefers Paris to Eden; "the terrestrial paradise is where I am."[34]

It is clear, then, that the author of *The Man of the World* is among those who believe they were put in the world to live in it, and to transform it into the kind of place in which one can live as comfortably as possible. Civilized living literally means city living. That Voltaire would differ so radically from someone like Jean-Jacques Rousseau with his glorification of natural man and his desire to return to nature is not in the least surprising. As time passed, Voltaire's philosophy of life would deepen, and he would reject the early optimism of his youth, the spirit of which is present in this poem, but he would never reject the world or find its pleasures anything but enjoyable. He never lost the gusto for luxurious living even when he was an aged sage at Ferney rather than a passionate young aesthete in Paris.

VII   *The Sphere of Human Happiness:*
Discourses in Verse on Man *(1738)*

The view of life expressed briefly in *The Man of the World* Voltaire soon developed further as a part of an overall philosophy of human happiness. This he presented in one of his longest and most ambitious poetical works, the *Discourses in Verse on Man* (1738). His debts to Alexander Pope's earlier *Essay on Man* and to Nicolas Boileau's work are obvious, but Voltaire's work has merits of its own which spring from his wit, his fresh perspective, and his always lively style.

The poem is divided into seven discourses or sections, beginning with one entitled "On the Equality of Conditions" and ending with one "On True Virtue." In the first, Voltaire optimistically assumes what Ralph Waldo Emerson later was to formulate as the law of compensation. Good and bad circumstances are equally distributed throughout the world, no matter what are a person's individual social station and opportunities. Everyone is seeking happiness and seeking it with similar needs and chances of finding it. In the second discourse, Voltaire formulates clearly his belief that free will is the basic condition for the creation of human happiness. Here, as in his *Treatise on Metaphysics,* he argues that the true essence of a man's life is freedom; for without it he cannot "conceive, will, act, design." [35] If we lacked free will we would only be so many machines or a mass of predestined automatons endowed with thought, "tools of the Deity's despotic power." [36] (Later, when Voltaire had given up his belief in free will for a scientific determinism, he would find himself facing precisely such philosophical dilemmas.)

Having dealt with freedom, the poet turns in the third discourse to what he believes is one of the major obstacles to human happiness, envy. Taking a position which Arthur Schopenhauer in the next century would develop, Voltaire claims that envy of the happiness and achievements of others poisons the wellsprings of joy for a large part of mankind. The true genius, he holds, never knows envy.[37] He is too preoccupied with creation to have anything but admiration for the works of others. Envy is dangerous for most of us, however, because as an extreme emotion it draws us away from the path of moderation, which is the subject of the fourth discourse. "Fools by excess make varied pleasures pall," the philosopher poeticizes, "the wise man's moderate, and enjoys them all."[38] Here Voltaire's classical heritage, with its stress on the golden mean, clearly shines through. He sounds like a true Epicurean when he advises us to learn how to quit pleasure "for pleasure's sake." Pleasure is our natural end but when pursued excessively or solely it will lead to pain.

Pleasure is analyzed more fully in the fifth discourse. Here, as in *The Epistle to Urania*, Voltaire rejects religious doctrines and practices that counsel man to renounce all pleasure for some sort of supernatural salvation. God created man as a pleasure-seeking being; pleasures in themselves are good rather than evil; and men can seek their own pleasure without interfering with the pleasure-seeking of others or losing all sense of social responsibility. This discussion of pleasure is woven into the larger picture of the nature of man presented in the sixth discourse. Here, as in his remarks on Blaise Pascal's view of man in the *Philosophical Letters*, Voltaire rejects the pessimistic Christian conception of man. We should not go beyond the earthly sphere to presume to know with any finality the nature of man or of God. Nor should we be so presumptuous as to believe that God created the world for our pleasure. Given consciousness, a rat, a goose, or an ass looking at his reflection in the water might be equally convinced of its supposedly central place in the scheme of things. Voltaire simply advises us to "rest contented with our fate, and have faith that our bliss is suited to our present state."[39] We can believe and hope that "all is right" even if we cannot prove it. To hope for perfect happiness is foolish, but we can certainly make ourselves and our world happier if we concentrate on living here rather than postpone it in the expectation that we may live elsewhere in a supernatural realm. To be wise and virtuous means, in the poet's view, to be just, not austere. To be happy and blest, it is enough to "love God and love his creatures."[40]

The philosophy expressed in Voltaire's poetical discourses is consistent with that of his earlier poems. Happiness is to be found on earth rather than in heaven. To find it one must discard religious dogmas with their fixation on guilt, sin, and self-renunciation. Eventually his confident optimism would be shattered, his conviction in the basic goodness of man shaken, and his belief in free will discarded. But he would never discard natural religion for any sort of Christian revelation. God certainly exists, but He is not the tyrant of the universe. We are on our own and must make the most of it. This was and remained his belief.

VIII *The Light of Reason:* On Natural Law (1752)

Voltaire developed further his conception of a natural religion in a poem originally written for Frederick the Great entitled *On Natural Law* (1752). Its fundamental thesis is that God has implanted in us ideas of justice and conscience which form the natural and universal basis of all true morality and religion. At the merely human level, he argues, moral standards and religious practices may vary widely, but this does not mean there is no underlying unity which one may discover by rational reflection and moral sensitivity.

> "Morality, unvaried and the same,"
> Proclaims to each age God's holy name.
> 'Tis Trajan's law, 'tis Socrates', yours,
> By nature preached, like nature it endures;
> Reason receives it, and the keen remorse
> Of conscience strengthens it, and gives it force.[41]

The seeds of virtue have been sown in our heart, then, and we only have to cultivate them rationally and conscientiously to see them grow and flourish. Man-made laws may reflect the cultural norms and prejudices of their time, but the natural law transcends such limitations. Voltaire is making a distinction similar to that made by Immanuel Kant (though without the accompanying subtle epistemology and metaphysics of Kant) between empirical and rational conscience, the relative sense of obligation which is culturally conditioned and the absolute sense of obligation which is cross-cultural and universally binding. When one acts according to the inner natural law one is guided by the light of reason which illuminates the way of universal moral justice, truth, and goodness. Then, and then only, does one see that self-love and social love are not mutually exclusive but basically identical. As he had already suggested in his earlier poems, Voltaire sees no contradiction between egoism and altruism.

From this general perspective on the nature of natural law, the philosophical poet turns to some implications in the realms of the sacred and secular. When humans fail to refer to reason as a sanction of moral and religious feeling, they can easily go astray and fall victim to irrational appeals which claim that one religion or moral code has a monopoly on truth. This can lead to gross injustices and iniquities all perpetuated in the name of true (actually false) religion. Catholics then can "conscientiously" persecute Protestants, and Protestants can discriminate against Catholics. Everywhere religious fanatics cry out to their opponents: "Wretch, think like me, or else this moment die!" [42]

When he discusses the importance of accepting a natural or rational law rather than a dogmatic authority, Voltaire is discussing something that drastically affects whether humans will live happily or miserably on earth. Religious wars, Voltaire believes, are the result of pious rage. They would never arise if men did not at times withdraw their allegiance from nature's laws for laws framed in the narrow limits of human imperfections. In Flanders the Armenians in the name of their faith were martyrs; in Holland they were executioners. Only adherence to the divine or natural law can provide the eternal wisdom needed to cool and temper human passions. "Religion well observed will quell your rage; and make you mild, compassionate and sage." [43]

With Frederick the Great—the benevolent and rational despot —in mind, Voltaire boldly asserts that, when crowned, kings take on a duty to maintain order and to treat all equally before this universal binding law. No one—kings, priests, or metaphysicians —should consider themselves above natural law.

IX   *Optimism Shattered:* Poem on the The Lisbon Earthquake *(1756)*

When Voltaire heard of the great earthquake in Lisbon which killed between thirty to forty thousand inhabitants on November 1, 1755, his response was as agonized as that of some thinkers in the twentieth century to the explosion of the first atomic bomb. He was shocked, horrified, and stunned. In this case nature, not man, was the villain responsible for the tragedy. Imagine Voltaire's rage when he soon heard theologians and philosophers trying to reconcile the loss of lives in the earthquake with some sort of divine plan! Somehow, they were claiming, it all had occurred in accord with a benevolent divine plan. "Whatever is, is right," they exclaimed, quoting Alexander Pope. "All is for the best, in this best of all possible worlds," they argued, repeating Leibniz, so somehow the earthquake was good rather than evil.

The various rationalizations were as ingenious as they were unconvincing. Perhaps the people killed were sinners who deserved their fate. Perhaps God was teaching others by this example a moral lesson. Perhaps God was taking the dead "to his bosom" in reward for their piety. And so on *ad infinitum.* Voltaire rejected all these arguments as absurd. In addition, he considered them to be travesties on a truly good God Who would not punish the guilty and the innocent alike; Who would not intervene in natural events to show His own power; and Who would certainly never be capable of acting to prove or to justify some obscure and self-centered metaphysical scheme.

The poem in which Voltaire expressed his initial shock, his continued perplexity, and his rage at those who attempted to rationalize the event is one of his greatest and most influential achievements as a thinker and as a poet. In his *Poem on the Lisbon Earthquake* (1756) he sounded the death knell for optimism. Later, in *Candide* he would bury it. The author gave his own interpretation of his famous poem in its preface:

If, when Lisbon, Moquinxa, Tetuan, and other cities were swallowed up with a great number of their inhabitants in the month of November, 1755, philosophers had cried out to the wretches, who with difficulty escaped from the ruins, "all this is productive of general good; the heirs of those who have perished will increase their fortune; masons will earn money by rebuilding the houses, beasts will feed on the carcasses buried under the ruins; it is the necessary effect of necessary causes; your particular misfortune is nothing, it contributes to universal good," such a harangue would doubtless have been as cruel as the earthquake was fatal, and all that the author of the poem upon the destruction of Lisbon has said amounts only to this.[44]

Voltaire rejects, then, all the rationalizations which might be given of the tragic event, most of which are based on the assumption that the earthquake must be seen as necessary in conformity to universal natural law or as right in conformity with the omnipotence and benevolence of God. Such "optimism" is really a kind of pessimism and fatalism in disguise. If this is the *best* of all possible worlds, what would the worst be like! No, it is far better and fairer to admit that the earthquake was evil; that it did cause real and great suffering which was essentially meaningless; and that the horror of the event cannot and should not be reconciled with the existence and nature of an all-good, all-powerful God. To explain away the disaster denies to each human being—"wretched man, earth-fated to be cursed"—the reality and dignity of his or her suffering and robs the person of the pity and assistance which should be elicited by the event. Voltaire himself prefers not to propose solutions to questions about the earthquake's meaning which transcended human understanding and related to ultimate human destiny. "Mysteries like these can no man penetrate,/ Hid from his view remains the book of fate." [45]

The poem ends, however, on a seemingly more encouraging note. While we are deceived if we believe that all now is well, we can at least have the consolation of believing that all may be well. We can be humble, bearing pain bravely without questioning Providence or trying to solve problems that confound our finite minds. "Man's sole bliss below" is hope.[46]

After Voltaire had expressed his response to the Lisbon earthquake in this poem, which moved all of Europe, his philosophy of life was altered and enriched. He had now recognized fully the reality of evil. He could never return to the easy optimism of his youth and gloss over suffering with the lackadaisical attitude of a happy hedonist.

X *Man of the Theater*

During his lifetime Voltaire wrote more than fifty plays in
verse, beginning with *Oedipus* (1718), written when he was less
than twenty and concluding with *Irène* (1778), which was produced in Paris shortly before his death at eighty-three. His career
as dramatist began with a play cast in a strictly classical mold
but filled with youthful defiance of authority and love of freedom,
and ended with a "tearful tragedy" imbued with the love of
mankind and devotion to tolerance that were characteristic of his
later philosophy of life. Voltaire retained throughout his life a
devotion to all things that had to do with theater, not only with
playwriting but also with acting, directing, and set design. Wherever he lived, he was not content unless he had his own theater
in which to produce his plays. He himself delighted in playing
parts in his own private productions. He found his first recognition in a theater as a young man and attained his "apotheosis"
in one as an aged sage.

Although Voltaire wrote comedies as well as tragedies, it was
primarily as a tragedian and as an epic poet that he attained
greatest celebrity in his century. To those who today think of him
as a master of wit and as a great writer of *contes* this seems
puzzling. Why did he make no lasting achievement to comedy?
Did he lack the objectivity to be another Molière? Did he lack
the ambition because of his desire to be another Racine? Did he
think of comedy as a mode of dramatic expression inferior to
tragedy? Did his humor perhaps find adequate outlet in other
forms of self-expression—for example, in his correspondence, in
his poetical satires, and in his philosophical tales? Whatever the
explanation, the "tearful comedies" that Voltaire wrote—the most
popular were *The Scotchman, The Prodigal,* and *Nanine*—are
considered to be inferior to his tragedies and today are forgotten.[47]

Those scholars who have traced the development of Voltaire's
tragedies find their sources not only in his preoccupation with his
great seventeenth-century French predecessors but also in the
influence of English models, notably John Dryden's sentimental
dramas or "tearful tragedies" with which Voltaire had become
acquainted during his sojourn in England. T. W. Russell, in his
important work *Voltaire, Dryden, and Heroic Tragedy,* holds that

Voltaire's program for the reform of French theater was to follow
in the trail already blazed by Dryden, "to give epic elevation to
tragedy by infusing a moral lesson, by portraying grandiose
events, and by heightening the style." [48] Voltaire was also following the best critical opinion of his time in seeing epic and tragedy
as the narrative and dramatic forms of heroic poetry.[49] In *The
Henriade* he had tried the epic or narrative mode of poetic expression. In his *Oedipus* and in his other tragedies he explored
the tragic or dramatic mode which seemed more in accord with
his talents, opportunities, and inclinations. His basically epic
imagination found satisfaction and fulfillment in the poetry of his
tragedies and later in the prose of his histories. In both of these
he also increasingly performed his self-appointed function as a
"legislator of mankind," to use the phrase of Percy Bysshe
Shelley, another poet-philosopher-propagandist.

XI   *Theory and Practice of a Tragedian*

To understand Voltaire's tragedies fully it would be necessary
not only to read and (whenever possible) to see them, but also
to read what their author had to say about them and about
tragedy in general in his prefaces, letters, and other works. From
these it is clear that for Voltaire a tragedy is more than just a
well-made play conforming (as far as possible) to the laws of
good dramatic writing. A dramatist may choose a subject appropriate to tragedy, skillfully contrive a plot or "invent an
intricate intrigue and unravel it," handle character properly and
write dialogue in verse convincingly, and still misfire as a
tragedian.[50] What more is necessary? The essential thing: to
affect strongly the emotions of the audience. "A poet should, as it
were, hold the hearts of spectators in his hand," Voltaire advises;
"he should wring the most obdurate hearts." [51] Following Aristotle, Voltaire places the emotions of pity and fear as central to
the tragic effect, but interprets them in a more practical and overt
sense as terror and sympathy. The successful writer of tragedies
must not be content simply to arouse the feelings of his audience;
he must reduce it to tears. Voltaire's idea of a successful night
at the theater is one in which there was neither an empty seat
nor a dry eye in the house. "The ultimate test of excellence in
composition and performance is, therefore," as R. S. Ridgway
puts it, "quite simple: one counts hankerchiefs." [52]

To make an audience weep is, of course, not enough, Voltaire recognizes; one must give them something worth weeping about. To provide emotional outlet *and* moral uplift are both important to achieving the highest tragic effect in the theater. In his early tragedies, those concerned with Greek and Roman themes, Voltaire managed to achieve his effect without the usual dramatist's reliance upon love interests. Rather he relied upon the audience's willingness and even eagerness to believe that an unseen transcendent power inevitably punishes wrongdoers or transgressors of the moral law. He was proud at the time that he did not have to depend upon cheap theatrics or easy sentiments in order to achieve his dramatic effects. French theater, he believed, had been far too preoccupied, to its detriment, with romantic love. As a result, it had become "an eternal school of gallantry" displaying what was in his opinion "a sort of coquetry which has nothing of a tragic nature." [53] Could not tragedy exist without love? And exist pure and more powerfully?

Among his own plays in which he attempted to provide perfect tragedy without love was *Mérope* (1743). The action of the play revolves around the determination of Aegisthus, the son of the former king of Messenia, to revenge the murder of his father by Polyphontes, who has usurped the king's throne and plans to marry his widow, Aegisthus's mother Mérope. Returning in disguise to the palace after many years' absence, he is believed to have killed the missing prince (himself). Aegisthus is almost killed by Mérope who holds him responsible for her lost son's death. Discovering who he really is and determined to protect him from exposure, Mérope consents to marry Polyphontes. But Aegisthus succeeds in killing Polyphontes at the wedding and liberates Messenia from his tyranny. Voltaire has purposely chosen the dramatic situation that Aristotle himself had praised most highly, and he manages things so as to extract maximum emotion from that situation, and without relying at all on romantic love in order to elicit cataracts of tears.

Although he wrote plays that did not depend upon love as their central pivot, Voltaire did not propose, however, that love should be totally banished from tragedies; he was only concerned that when love was introduced it should be handled by the playwright so as to elicit tragic rather than merely romantic emotions. As he explained his position in a letter on tragedy to the Englishman Lord Bolingbroke, in tragedy love should arise naturally from the plot and not simply be brought in to elicit audience interest. "It should be a passion entirely tragical, considered as a weakness, and opposed by remorse," he writes.[54] To show how dangerous the emotion of love can be it should be shown as leading to misfortunes or to crimes, and to show that it is not invincible it should be depicted as being subdued by virtue.

This kind of love Voltaire presented in what is perhaps his best play, *Zaïre* (1732). Set in the time of the Crusades, this play recounts the complications that arise from the love of Orosman, the sultan of Jerusalem, and Zaïre, a captured Christian maiden who is a convert to Islam. When Zaïre discovers that she is the daughter of the enslaved Crusader Lusignan and the sister of Nerestan, a fanatical Christian, she is torn by her loyalty to them and her love for the sultan. Mistaking Zaïre's interest in Nerestan for love, Orosman in a fit of jealousy kills her, only to discover afterwards the truth, which causes him in an agony of remorse to kill himself. Having witnessed the Muslim's noble suffering, Nerestan's formerly fanatical spirit is tempered by empathy and sympathy. Love has led to uncontrolled feeling and terrible suffering but it has been instrumental in redemption, in transforming a fanatic into a more humane person. As one commentator puts it, "his enlarged vision represents a victory over bigotry, and Zaïre and Orosman seem to have died in a good cause." [55]

Voltaire's attitude toward love is thus directly related to his view of the highest aim of tragedy, which is basically a moral aim. "True tragedy," he holds, "is the school of virtue." The dramatist's purpose, then, should be at once aesthetic and didactic.

The only difference between a refined theatre and books of morality is that the instruction of the former is all in action, that it is more interesting, and heightened by the charms of an art intended to make earth and heaven happy, and which was therefore truly called the language of the gods.[56]

This moral commitment Voltaire expresses throughout his dramatic work. Sometimes it is such an integral part of a play, so organically fused with its characters, action, and theme that it increases the whole work's intensity, beauty, and relevance. Sometimes, unfortunately, it seems to be of such urgency to the author that he appears to have produced a work of art simply to propound it. It then transforms what portended to be a work of art into an instrument of propaganda, and the playwright becomes a polemicist rather than an artist. In a study of Voltaire's philosophical propaganda in his tragedies, R. S. Ridgway showed how overloaded were Voltaire's plays with the pet ideas of the *philosophe,* and concluded that eventually propaganda destroyed artistry.[57]

Fortunately Voltaire is not always at his worst. In one of his most popular tragedies, *Alzire* (1736), the ideational content is clear but does not destroy the total effectiveness of the work created. The theme is expressed in the contrasts the playwright makes between the cruel excesses perpetrated by the supposedly Christian Spaniards in their conquest of America and the noble spirit of the supposedly infidel Indians, and emphasizes truly religious ideals of tolerance, forgiveness, and compassion. The heroine of the drama is Alzire, an Indian princess who has been married to Gusman, the son of Alvarez, Spanish governor of Peru. In the course of the play, Alzire is reunited with her brother Zamore, a young Indian leader who has been captured and tortured by Gusman, but she refuses to flee with him. Only after he has been fatally wounded by Zamore and has a chance to put to death both the Indian rebel and Alzire, does Gusman, astonished by Alzire's loyalty, love, and goodness, purge himself of hate and fanaticism and learn to practice genuine charity and forgiveness. Deeply moved by the changes in Gusman, Zamore is converted to his former enemy's religion. "I must indeed admire and love you," he exclaims as he falls at Gusman's feet.[58]

In the unlikely event that his audience (or readers) might have missed the moral implications, Voltaire made them later quite explicit in a preface to the play in which he states: "This tragedy . . . was written with a view of showing how far superior the spirit of true religion is to the light of nature." [59] What he really means is that it holds up his natural deist faith as superior to an unenlightened primitive religion and a dogmatic religion Christian in name only. He goes on to point out that barbarian and unconscious Christians are equally at fault when they rely upon rites and ceremonies while neglecting essential duties and concealing secret vices. Whether one offers up to pagan gods the blood of one's enemies or recites meaningless prayers to guarantee salvation makes no essential difference. The truly religious man, whether Christian or pagan, is the person who looks "upon all mankind as his brethen," does "them all the good in his power and pardons their offenses." Gusman was such a man "at the hour of death and Alvarez during the whole course of his life." [60]

Mohammed or Fanaticism (1741) is another of Voltaire's tragedies which carries a heavy load of propaganda without being spoiled as a successful drama. As its subtitle suggests, this is a play about the havoc that can be wreaked in the lives of innocent persons when religious fanaticism is directed to promote the self-interest of a charismatic religious charlatan. To aggrandize himself, the character Mohammed in the play persuades a young worshipper, Seid, to assassinate one of the prophet's implacable enemies, the Sheik Zopire. In reward Seid is to receive the slave-girl Palmire, whom Mohammed secretly plans to keep for himself. After he has mortally wounded the aged Zopire, Seid discovers that the old man is his father and that Palmire is his sister. He tries to avenge himself on the prophet, but dies of poison before he can succeed. After denouncing Mohammed, Palmire stabs herself to death. Although he professes remorse, Mohammed is triumphant in the end. Underscoring his moral and didactic intentions in a later letter written to Frederick the Great, Voltaire writes of *Mohammed* that it was not his design "merely to represent a real fact . . . but above all . . . to show the horrid schemes which villainy can invent, and fanaticism put in practice." [61] Mohammed is, in his view, "no more than Tartuffe in arms." As author of this play, he hopes to warn "impressionable persons" to be on guard against "such fatal delusions" and blind obedience as those from which Seid suffered and which lead to such dreadful consequences. We should not follow blindly those who preach hate and encourage us to persecute those who differ from us. "A spirit of indulgence would make us all brothers; a spirit of persecution can create nothing but monsters." [62]

If Voltaire, for his own propagandistic purposes, unfairly transforms the historical figure of Mohammed into a paradigm of evil and a perpetuator of fanaticism, he does this not because he is ignorant of the historical Mohammed but for the sake of what was to him a higher purpose. A tragedy is not a history but a work of art intended to move and to improve. He is depicting not what men are but what they ought to be or ought not to be. Throughout his works, as he proudly pointed out, he "endeavored to enforce that humanity which ought to be the distinguishing characteristic of a thinking being." [63] His tragedies, like his other works, give expression to "a desire to promote the happiness of all men, and an abhorrence of injustice and oppression." [64] If this means making the historical Mohammed a diabolic figure driving humanity on to destruction, such a transformation is justifiable in order to enlighten mankind to the dangers of religious fanaticism and to aid in crushing that "infamous thing."

In the case of *Mohammed,* the transformation worked as art, but Voltaire was not always so fortunate, especially as increasingly the usually critical artist became subservient to the committed sage. In one of his least known plays, *Socrates,* the fifth-century philosopher has been transmogrified into an eighteenth-century deist who is made to speak such lines as these when he is defending himself against charges brought against him by crafty sophists and malevolent priests:

I say, there is but one God, in his nature infinite . . . one great architect, one sole master, and preserver . . . the first of beings, the one incomprehensible, incommunicable being, the eternal, all-just, and all-powerful God.[65]

This "Socrates," like his creator Voltaire, urges his fellow countrymen to "be careful above all not to turn religion into metaphysics." The essence of true religion is morality; one should not dispute about it but simply worship the supreme God. "Socrates" could well have taken his lines directly from Voltaire's *Philosophical Dictionary;* he is certainly no longer the true philosopher of Plato's *Dialogues.* Later, when he has been condemned and is in prison awaiting death, he replies to his disciple Crito's exclamation about "this legal murder": "thus it is that men will often behave to the worshippers of one true God, and the enemies of superstition." [66]

Thus Socrates, like many of the other characters in Voltaire's later dramas, becomes a mouthpiece for his own religious and philosophical ideas. A study of his development as a tragedian is interesting if only to see how the *philosophe* steadily co-opted the artist in Voltaire as it also co-opted the philosopher and historian. Whether he was writing a play, a *conte,* a philosophical treatise, or a history, Voltaire considered it his duty to promote the efforts of humanity in its struggle for enlightenment.

XII   *Defunct Dramatist*

Of a contemporary poet's "Ode to Posterity" Voltaire once remarked facetiously that he doubted if it would ever reach its destination. The same might have been said of his innumerable poetical dramas, which were extravagantly praised in his day, and compared favorably with the chief enduring works of ancient and modern times; not one today is treasured in posterity's permanent repertory. Occasionally a tragedy by Voltaire is revived in Paris by the Comédie française perhaps to show that it can be done or as an act of Gallic patriotism. Then, and only then, does one have a chance to see what can be done on stage with a Voltaire script. Before and after, we must be content, if we are so inclined, only to read *Zaïre, Mérope, Mohammed,* and *The Orphan of China,* some of Voltaire's greatest successes when they first appeared. Some students of his plays, however, still defend their worth, and bemoan their neglect today. One of the ablest of these, Jack R. Vrooman, thinks that Voltaire's century rightly had a high regard for his plays, and that they can still bring pleasure and instruction if we give them a chance. "As tragedy," Vrooman writes, "they present a different but nonetheless coherent view of man's repeated failure to achieve happiness." [67] He also thinks that they can still work as drama to stir emotion and stimulate intelligence. And "as art," he continues, "they remain dynamic."

Whether a revived Voltaire would be a vital Voltaire is still, then, a debatable question. No one would deny, however, that his plays certainly remain of permanent historical importance in the understanding of Voltaire, his times, and the history of the French theater. As plays they are at least melodramatic monuments of an era in French literary history which was virtually devoid of true tragedy. Modern readers or listeners of these plays will probably continue to find their language stilted, their plots overly contrived, their characters unconvincing, their emotion excessive, their themes unoriginal, their philosophy shallow, and their author's point of view excessively moralistic. This is only to say, according to some defenders of Voltaire's dramas, simply that they are not to our present-day taste.

In his own day Voltaire was considered to be not only a master craftsman of tragedy whose works could rival those of his great predecessors, Corneille and Racine, but also was viewed as in some respects a daring innovator in theater. While this "new Sophocles" was valiantly trying to preserve the so-called classical unities, the properly sublime verse style, and the traditional five-acter, he was also bringing about changes in what one could and would see when one went to the theater. In some respects his novelties were technical.[68] For example, he cleared the stage of the benches on which traditionally privileged spectators sat. By introducing "living tableaux" he made the theatrical spectacle more striking to the eye. He tried to make the dialogue sound more natural while at the same time heightening its poetical appeal. And so on.

But his more important contributions to reforming the drama of his time had to do with his choice of characters, settings, and themes. He did not hesitate to introduce characters not just from ancient history but from recent French history as heroes in his tragedies. He entranced his audiences by presenting plays that were not just set in Rome or Athens, but in exotic parts of the East and of the New World. *Zaïre* took them to Jerusalem, *Mohammed* to Mecca, *Semiramis* to Assyria, and *Alzire* to Peru. He instructed his audience and flattered their intelligence by introducing philosophical ideas into his dramas, embodying them in characters who were committed to live and usually to die for them.

Most important of all, Voltaire gave his audiences an emotional experience when they came to see one of his plays. As R. S. Ridgway pointed out, Voltaire was "less of a 'literary' dramatist than an eminently practical man of the theatre with audience reaction uppermost in his mind," and his popularity "may be summed up in one word: emotion." [69] In Voltaire's emphasis on the emotional impact of drama, he was also, unknowingly, breaking ground for the Romanticist playwrights. He would have agreed with Victor Hugo's pronouncement that the theater is a cathedral of the spirit in which souls are formed. As a dramatist Voltaire may have died, but as an influence on the theater he lives on.

XIII *Voltaire's Living Poetry*

Although Voltaire always thought of himself as first and foremost a poet, he was not the poet he thought he was. Fortunately, he was a poet of another sort. Today the epic, philosophical, and dramatic poetry upon which his fame as a poet rested are seldom read for the sheer pleasure of reading poetry. The neoclassical forms in which these works were cast today seem artificial and restrictive. They have long since lost most of their power to inspire reflection or express emotion; they may have once worked for Voltaire's audiences but they leave most of us cold. They are important monuments of a long-gone era and important to the understanding of that era, but unlike the great poetry of the past they are no longer capable of functioning as objective correlatives to elicit and express emotions. They are mummies of formerly living forms, remains of Voltaire's once flourishing poetical activity.

If we are to find a living poetry in Voltaire, we must look for it elsewhere than in his "works of grandeur." For, ironically, Voltaire was often at his worst when he thought he was at his best. As the French literary critic Gustave Lanson pointed out, the value of his poetry usually is inversely proportional to the grandeur of his poetical form. One should look for the poet in Voltaire, then, not in his big productions but in his little works, in his lighter rather than in his heavier works, in his "fugitive works" in which we can catch the poet on the wing. There one finds a Voltaire who is a true poet, a worthy companion of the other, still living Voltaire we know. As Ralph Arthur Nablow writes in a recent study of Voltaire's lighter verse, "the less formal poems shed an illuminating light on Voltaire's many-sided character, revealing him in his more frequent role as an enlightened thinker and ironic observer of society, and in his less-known role as a man of true feeling, appreciative of the less cerebral aspects of life and sensitive to its poetic qualities." [70]

To get to know this virtually unknown Voltaire will bring to the student of his work as well as to all lovers of poetry rare and unexpected pleasure. This is the Voltaire who could write nostalgically to a former mistress a poem so perfectly expressive of the changes that time can bring to love as his *Epistle of 'you' and of 'thou.'* The Voltaire who could write in *From Love to Friendship:*

> If you would have me love once more,
> The blissful age of love restore;
> From wine's free joys, and lovers' cares,
> Relentless time, who no man spares,

> Urges me quickly to retire,
> And no more to such bliss aspire.[71]

This true poet could express in one poem the exuberance he felt upon first arriving in the beautiful countryside near Lake Geneva ("O house of Aristippus! O gardens of Epicurus!").[72] In another poem he can capture the tranquility of a life lived close to nature ("How sweet it is to spend the decline of one's days as the great Virgil spent his spring!").[73] In different moods he could find the poetical means for consoling an ageing beauty who "even in her life's decline, outshone others in their spring," [74] or for summing up in verse the requisites to happiness, beginning with these lines:

> A man must think, or else the brute
> May his superior worth dispute;
> A man must love, for were it not
> For love, most hard would be his lot.[75]

The range of this happy poet's interest is as wide as it is various. He will take the time to advise in verse a newly married couple not to love each other too much, as "that is the surest way to love each other for ever." [76] Or he will put into poetical form more effectively some of the same critical judgments that are found elsewhere in his works. Of Blaise Pascal, for example, he mused poetically that "He taught men to hate themselves; I should like, in spite of him, to teach them to love one another." [77]

Voltaire, personal poet, can often illuminate in the deepest sense his own life as well as ours. The intensity with which he loved Emilie du Châtelet, not just as a mistress but as a person, is revealed anew in the epistle he wrote to his competitor for that love, the poet St. Lambert, which concludes with the vision of "our astronomic Emily descending from her aphelion, wearing an old black apron, her hand still stained with ink" but soon recapturing her charms. "Take quickly to her dressing table these flowers," he advises his fellow poet, " . . . and sing her on your pipes the lovely airs rehearsed by Love, and unknown to Newton." [78] In old age he would express his profoundest feelings about life in other verse epistles such as that *To Horace* (1772) in which he addresses the poet as an old friend:

> I am writing to you today, voluptuous Horace,
> To you who breathe the softness and the grace,
> Who, facile in your verse, and gay in your discourse,
> Sing the sweet pleasures, the wines, and the loves . . .[79]

And, finally, in his very last poem, written shortly before his death in 1778, in which he bade farewell to life, he begins "Adieu; I am going into that country whence never returned my late father." [80]

In poetry such as this Voltaire reached the heights of emotion and of thought characteristic of true poetry. Here, and not in the loftiness of *The Henriade* or in the grandly expressed emotions of *Zaïre* he realized his nature as a poet who could record for himself and posterity something of permanent value in language that is clear, elegant, and permeated with rhythmic feeling. He had defined poetry as "the music of the soul and above all of great and of feeling souls." In his so-called lighter verse he proved that he could do more than define or fake poetry; he could write it.

CHAPTER 3

Making History by Writing It:
Voltaire as Historian

I The First Modern Historian

VOLTAIRE'S interest in history began in his student days, when he studied the Greek and Roman historians, biblical history, and the history of France. It developed into active research while he was writing his epic poem on Henry IV, which Ira Wade has called, "history in rhyme." [1] Many of his dramas were also firmly rooted in historical research. His first essay in history dealt with the civil wars in France during the time of Henry IV. This was written in England, the country that supposedly changed him from a poet into a philosopher, and it was also in England that he started his first bona fide history in prose, *Charles XII* (1731). After that success, Voltaire later wrote a number of historical works, the most important of which were *The Age of Louis XIV* (1751) and *Essay on the Customs and the Spirit of Nations* (1756). His appointment as Royal Historiographer in 1745 gave him direct access to a mass of source materials upon which he could base further works, including the important *Age of Louis XV* (1769). Throughout his life he continued to read and write history, which was always closely intertwined with his other creative endeavors, especially with his dramas. His last historical work, *History of the Parliament of Paris* (1769), brought his readers right up into the times in which they were living. By the time he died he was widely hailed as Europe's greatest historian. Today he is often referred to as "the first modern historian." [2]

"One hesitates to class Voltaire as an historian," a recent biographer writes, "he was an event. If he wrote history, it was because he meant to make it." [3] Whether or not Voltaire deserves to be called the first modern historian, he certainly contributed much to the making and remaking of history as we know it today. Before Voltaire showed how history could and should be written it was, in his opinion, far from modern to say the least. Fact and fable were often so confused in it that the reader could seldom get a clear idea of what had actually happened. "Imagination alone," Voltaire believed, "wrote the first histories." [4] Often a host of irrelevant (though often entertaining) anecdotes diverted the reader's attention or extensive chronologies lulled him to sleep. Kings, priests, politicians, and generals dominated the story, and little if any attention was given to artists, scientists, and sages— to what is today called "intellectual history." Events were recounted, sometimes in elaborate detail, but their causes were seldom if ever satisfactorily explained. The hand of God was all too often glimpsed behind the scenes, operating the levers of the historical machinery. At times it seemed as though no absurdity were too absurd for an historian to believe and—worse still—to report as true. Of course, a few fairly reliable histories, both ancient and modern, were available, and Voltaire himself gratefully relied upon them, but only after the most careful scrutiny. This cautious critical attitude was itself, Voltaire liked to think, characteristically modern.

Being a modern historian was by no means an easy task, as Voltaire saw it. First of all, it entailed being comprehensive. "Modern historians are expected to provide more details, more attested facts, precise dates and authorities, and to give more attention to customs, laws, manners, commerce, finance, agriculture and population." [5] In the modern era, the scope of history, like that of mathematics and physics, he recognized, had increased tremendously. To meet this challenge Voltaire undertook what was by his contemporaries' standards an enormous amount of research into primary and secondary sources. As an historian he had to know; and to know, in his view, meant to know everything that could be known. To do this, or even to aspire to it, meant that he had to be far more than an historian; he had to be a philosopher in the sense in which Francis Bacon defined it, one who takes all of knowledge as his sphere. So well did he do this that a recent historian claims that he was "a thinker who amassed probably more accurate information about the world in all its aspects than any man since Aristotle." [6]

Knowing everything not only suggested a goal to Voltaire as a modern historian but also a method. The method was scepticism.

The historian should practice what was then called the Pyrrhonism of history, the careful and critical doubting that preceded tentative judgment or suspension of belief. This sceptical method, long before Voltaire, had been used by French philosophers, notably by Montaigne, Descartes, Bayle, and Fontenelle, all of whom Voltaire had read and assimilated. It meant that a thinker should have (as Friedrich Nietzsche later put it) not just the courage of his convictions but the courage to question his convictions. Incredulity, then, Voltaire urged, should be the foundation of historical knowledge.[7] Probability, not absolute certainty, should be the historian's aim. Truth-claims should be brought before the tribunal of reason, experience, and common sense and forced to defend themselves. The historian will have to become an expert in sifting, sorting, rejecting, and evaluating evidence. He will learn to be suspicious not only of historical records and documents but also of monuments, coins, metals, and inscriptions. He will even learn to be suspicious of himself—when he is not being sceptical.

Along with his striving for comprehensiveness and his reliance on a sceptical method in attaining historical truth, Voltaire was also modern in his approach as an historian in searching out the causes of events. Although he believed in God, he did not believe that God had any direct role in determining the direction or outcome of the course of history. He was a deist. God existed; God created the universe; but God, having created an orderly and well-running universe, did not and could not intervene in or interfere with the natural or human course of events. Adhering to such a world view, which he considered to be strictly modern and scientific—"based irrefutably on Newton"—Voltaire never sought or expected to encounter supernatural causes in his study of history. Instead he looked for natural and human causes—such as the operation of climate, political institutions, and religion—which influenced history. Like the Baron de Montesquieu, he was naturalistic in his approach.

But Voltaire tried to go deeper than others had in probing the *modus operandi* of historical events. He wanted to grasp the ideas that motivated human conduct individually and collectively. Ideas to him were as important as facts in understanding what had happened in history. That is why in his most ambitious work, his *Essay on the Customs and the Spirit of Nations*, he devoted so much attention to the merging and the unifying of the beliefs, values, and practices that characterized different cultures and gave them their unique definition and direction. If there is progress in the history of the world—and Voltaire was convinced that there is—it has come about by the efforts of great men to promote the highest ideals of reason, tolerance, and compassion which have emerged in humanity's never-ceasing striving toward enlightenment.

II *Giving Form to History*

While Voltaire was thus redefining the content and approach of modern history, he was equally concerned with form. "There are laws for writing history as there are for all the creative arts; there are plenty of precepts, but very few great artists." [8] Although he never specified what these laws were, as one of the few great artists, he gave several examples of how he practiced them. He did state that "a grave, pure, varied, and pleasant style is needed." [9] And he compared briefly the structuring of a history to the structuring of a tragedy. We do know that his contemporaries were struck with the newness and unique qualities of his histories, and were delighted with their liveliness, clarity, and informativeness. As Lord Chesterfield put it, "Bolingbroke has just taught me how history should be read, Voltaire shows me how it should be written." [10] The modern historian Ferdinand Schevill believed that Voltaire's "primary achievement was to reestablish history as a branch of literature and thus to raise it once more to the rank it had held among the ancients." [11] Whether or not this achievement outweighed his others, Voltaire did write modern history in a modern style for modern readers. And as Hippolyte Taine pointed out, "as a simplifier and popularizer, he had no rival in the world." [12]

III *The Historian as Moralist*

There is a final and important feature of Voltaire as an historian that is not modern and that, to some contemporary critics, seriously flaws his reputation and achievement. He was a moralist. History, in his view, is ultimately valueless if it is not put to some good use. Like civics, it can teach citizens their duties and rights, at least indirectly. By drawing and implying comparisons between the laws and customs of his own country and other countries, the historian can suggest to his readers ways that should be emulated or avoided. Further, historians can and should hold out the belief or hope that things might have been different in the past and may be different in the future. To be sure, it sometimes might seem as though chance and necessity rather than human will determine the course of history, but Voltaire firmly believes that basically history is created by men rather than by luck, fate, or gods.

He is an optimist at least in the sense that an optimist believes the future to be uncertain—not already determined. "The crimes and misfortunes of history cannot be too frequently pondered on," he writes, "for whatever people say, it is possible to prevent both." [13] He would have agreed that he who ignores or is ignorant of the errors committed in the past may be doomed to repeat them. "Destroy the study of history and you would very possibly see St. Bartholomew's Days in France and Cromwells in England," he warns.[14] (The study of the Holocaust is often justified by some today on similar grounds.) History may have been bad —"debacles, disasters, and deaths"—but it would have been even worse had there been no historians. This deep conviction— that the historian is not just a recorder, a narrator, an artist but also a moral judge—lies at the very heart of Voltaire's practice. This may not seem modern, as it may not seem modern in the case of some later historians—Albert Schweitzer and Arnold Toynbee, for example—but it must be taken into account in reading Voltaire's histories. Like Lord Bolingbroke, he never doubted that "history is philosophy [i.e., morality] teaching by examples." [15]

If one reads Voltaire's histories in order, it will become apparent that as his knowledge, maturity, and goals broadened his historical perspective became wider and more philosophical. If, as Emerson claimed, "there is properly no history, only biography," then Voltaire's career as a philosopher-historian began with a biography of a man *(History of Charles XII),* continued with a biography of an era *(The Age of Louis XIV),* and culminated with a biography of a world *(Essay on the Customs and the Spirit of Nations).* Although he wrote other histories along the way, these are the only ones that really matter today and that will be briefly considered here.

IV   *"Half Alexander, Half Don Quixote":*
The History of Charles XII *(1731)*

Voltaire's choice of Charles XII of Sweden (1682–1718) as the
subject of his first major historical work was a stroke of genius.
Here was a military leader who had only recently turned most
of Europe upside down by his grandiose ambition, his reckless
courage, and unpredictable strategems. Charles was a "wild
warrior king" whose love of glory ruined both him and his
country; an enigmatic character whose ill-starred career attracted
romantic interest; a madman perhaps, but a madman with a
sublime purpose. At a later date Voltaire might have chosen a
Napoleon or a Rommel to suit his ends as historian; in his day
there could have been no more colorful or challenging subject
than the one he chose.

His imagination fired by the image of King Charles and his
tragicomic career, the ambitious young historian set out to ex-
ploit fully his material, just as he had done previously when
writing about the trials and triumphs of Henry IV of France.
Voltaire's interest in the Swedish king lay not so much in his
inner personality—for, after all, the materials there were scanty
and Voltaire was no psychologist—but rather in the man of
action. As a biographer of this man, he wanted to reveal how his
actions shaped not just his own destiny but also the destiny of
nations. As a literary artist and dramatist writing history, he
wanted to give a satisfying and appropriate aesthetic form to his
rich and complex subject matter. Histories, he believed, should
be as carefully constructed and well written as tragedies, and
like tragedies they should have their expositions, complications,
and *dénouements.* The drama of Charles could be viewed as a
drama in which a high-minded and single-purposed character
seeks, above all, glory for himself and his country. Uncompromising and unweening in his ambition, this protagonist is finally
cut down amidst the wreck and ruin which he has brought upon
himself and his countrymen. As in *Oedipus,* the subject of Voltaire's first play, hubris does not go unpunished.

At the same time that he was viewing the story of Charles in
dramatic terms, Voltaire was also viewing it in moralistic terms.
While in writing his history he was depicting "extraordinary
events," relating them to "the most extraordinary man" that ever
lived, he considered this to be a "trifling pleasure" compared

with the higher end toward which he as an historian was aspiring. Faithful to Lord Bolingbroke's maxim, he employed the history of Charles to teach philosophy (i.e., morality) through examples. Charles, he maintained, is an example to all rulers of how a king's unchecked ambition can ruin a kingdom. "No king, surely," he stated in the preliminary discourse to *Charles XII*, "can be so incorrigible as, when he reads *The History of Charles XII*, not to be cured of the vain ambition of making conquests." [16] If a leader so skilled, so well endowed financially, so strong militarily, failed in his conquests, should not other would-be conquerors, Voltaire asked, curb their ambitions in light of Charles's unfortunate fate?

These literary and moralistic aspirations of the young historian help to account for the book's nature and appeal. It is exceptionally well written so that the wider significance of its character's struggles are never lost sight of in the wealth of specific historical detail. Despite his enigmatic qualities, the character of Charles emerges clearly enough to tantalize the imagination. As an English historian writes, "the person of Charles XII stands out from the text as if he had been etched in steel." [17] If this is so, it is due not just to Voltaire's consummate skill in narrating the events in his protagonist's career—his blitzkrieg attacks on his enemies, his amazing victories and sudden reversals of fortune, his total unwillingness to admit defeat—but to other skills as well. Voltaire has thoroughly researched the life and exploits of Charles, reading a vast amount of primary and secondary sources as well as talking with numerous "eye-witnesses of undoubted veracity" to the events described.[18] He could rightly be proud in assuring his reader that if ever a history merited his trust, this one did. Later historians have for the most part found Voltaire's pride in his work justified. For, along with the prodigious amount of research which he put into the writing of *Charles XII*, he maintained throughout his critical attitude toward his sources, weighing, sifting, evaluating, and selecting them with the utmost care in his search for their "truth."

The enduring value of *Charles XII* as a work of history as well as a work of art must be insisted upon, since it has been cavalierly dismissed by some contemporary readers because "it reads just like a novel" (the implication being that it therefore must be only fictionalized history). Voltaire showed here, as he was also to show in his later historical works, that history did not have to be written in a dry or tedious manner in order to be good history.

He wanted to write about modern subjects in a modern manner for the instruction and enjoyment of a wide variety of readers.

This point having been made, we can still recognize that the enjoyment to be found in reading *Charles XII* today will probably lie in Voltaire's skill as an artist rather than an historian. His dramatization in this book of the monumental struggle between two great leaders, Charles "the Invincible" of Sweden and Peter "the Great" of Russia, still rivets attention, portraying Charles as the symbol of a waning empire; Peter as the symbol of a new era. Voltaire's schoolboy love of heroes and grand events shines through as he sets the stage for his account of the pivotal battle between his two sharply contrasted heroes:

It was on the eighth of July, 1709, that the decisive battle of Poltava was fought between the two most famous monarchs that were then in the world. Charles XII, illustrious for nine years of victories; Peter Alexiowitz for nine years of pain taken to form troops equal to those of Sweden: the one glorious for having given away dominions; the other for having civilized his own; Charles, fond of dangers, and fighting for glory alone; Alexiowitz scorning to fly from danger, and never making war but from interested views: the Swedish monarch liberal from an innate greatness of soul; the Muscovite never granting favors but in order to serve some particular purpose: the former a prince of uncommon sobriety and continence, naturally magnanimous, and never cruel but once; the latter having not yet worn off the roughness of his education, or the barbarity of his country, as much the object of terror to his subjects as of admiration to strangers, and too prone to excesses, which even shortened his days.[19]

Peter's defeat of Charles in this battle provides Voltaire with the turning point of his entire account of the fortunes of the Swedish king, whom he characterized most succinctly as "half Alexander, half Don Quixote." [20]

But Voltaire is doing more than formulating a turning point or contrasting two characters; he is contrasting two different mentalities, two different possible ways of life, one representing the old and irrational hold of the past, the other the new and rational promise of the future. Peter's history (which Voltaire would pursue in detail in a later work) was just beginning as Charles's ended when, in the midst of a siege, he was killed by a stray bullet. This brings the drama to a conclusion. Having witnessed the sudden death of the king, one of his taciturn officers remarks to his fellows: "Come, gentlemen, the farce is ended, let us now go to supper." [21] Here, as elsewhere, Voltaire the artist is in careful control of his materials and medium. In a study of how Voltaire transformed history into art in *Charles XII*, Lionel Gossman compares the book to a picaresque mock-epic having as its hero the Swedish king. Throughout, Voltaire contrasts the "fantastical exploits" of Charles with the "sober purposefulness" of Peter the Great. Continuing, Gossman writes:

The brilliant arpeggios of the right hand are constantly being punctuated, opposed and commented on by the more somber notes of the bass. This play of contrasts gives to the work an underlying dramatic structure and a greater comprehensiveness than it would otherwise have had. It makes of Charles XII not just the story of an extraordinary man, but the drama—somewhat ·schematized, it is true—of an age.[22]

While it would be reading too much into the work to see in it Voltaire's later philosophical ideas, it would not be difficult to find embodied in Charles the spirit of unquestioned authority, self-glorification, and fanatical pursuit of goals in contrast to the spirit of criticism, altruism, and enlightenment which Peter at least partially embodied and which Voltaire sought to promote increasingly in his own life and works. In any case, while we can be sure that Voltaire found much to admire in Charles—"he was the only man," he writes, "most certainly he was the only king, that ever lived without failings"—he rejected him as an ideal which should be emulated.[23] "He carried all the virtues of the hero to such an excess as to render them no less dangerous than the opposite vices." This is the final judgment of the young dramatist-turned-historian-moralist. To this he adds: "From the history of his life, however, succeeding kings may learn that a quiet and happy government is infinitely preferable to so much glory." [24]

If Voltaire expected this moral message to be heeded by the then-ruling king of France, Louis XV, for whom it was probably intended, he was sorely disappointed. When *Charles XII* appeared in 1731, it was seized by government authority as possibly damaging to France's foreign relations. If the king himself read the book there is no evidence that he profited from it; his record as a ruler is overwhelmingly to the contrary. Nevertheless, Voltaire's confidence in the power and authority of the historian

remained unshaken, and *Charles XII* gave dazzling testimony to
that. As he somewhat condescendingly pointed out there, the
historian as the preserver of the race's memory wields great power
over those who consider themselves to be the "makers of history." [25] He reminded rulers that they are publicly accountable
for their conduct, and that if they wished to enjoy a favorable
opinion among mankind and among historians they must strive to
promote public welfare and happiness rather than their selfish
interests.[26] For they can be assured that eventually they will be
judged by posterity and by history. The business of the historian
is, in his opinion, to record the truth, not to flatter. And to record
entails registering facts and achievements; but it also necessitates
judging morals and evaluating conduct, seeking the human meaning.

Such a self-confident and critical attitude on the part of an
historian toward his so-called superiors, the ruling class, must
have been shocking to those authorities who read the book with
a jaundiced eye. And they were not mistaken if they read slightly
subversive intentions between the lines. For even in Voltaire's
earliest historical work, *Charles XII*, the homunculus of the
philosophe was alive and kicking.

V   *Apotheosis of the Human Spirit:*
The Age of Louis XIV *(1751)*

"It is not simply the life of this prince that I am writing,"
Voltaire confided to a fellow historian while he was working on
his second great historical work, *The Age of Louis XIV,* "any
more than it is the annals of his reign; it is more the history of the
human spirit, drawn from the most glorious age of the human
spirit." [27] Thus the now-mature historian defined his task; to
describe not just the lives and actions of major historical figures
as he had done in *Charles XII,* but to present a panorama of an
entire age which to him was exemplified and dominated by one
paramount person, the Sun King of Versailles. For "no single
person," he held, "could epitomize the high level that European
civilization had reached in the late seventeenth century better
than Louis XIV." [28] Voltaire wanted to make it clear from the
start that he was not writing this history as a patriotic Frenchman
about the greatest of all French kings; he was writing it as a
philosophical historian concerned with the achievement and

destiny of the human race. The fullest revelation of this achievement would be found, he believed, not in the political intrigues
and military events of the time but rather in its intellectual and
artistic life. He was far more interested in what a great artistic
genius such as Racine had accomplished than in how many men
had been killed in an important battle. Louis was the hero of his
history not "only because of the good he has done to Frenchmen,
but because of the good he has done for mankind." [29] Louis deserved to be the focal point of his history not just because he was
king but because he was the stimulator and sustainer of the
values of civilization.

In the Introduction to his new work Voltaire explained briefly
his overall view of history, which justified, he believed, his
focusing attention on the age of Louis XIV.[30] There had been in
the history of the world, he claimed, only four happy ages in
which artistic perfection had been achieved and the human
spirit had reached its highest fulfillment and fruition. So far
these truly great ages had been: the Golden Age of Greece from
Pericles to Alexander; the Age of Julius Caesar and Augustus;
the Age of Renaissance Italy; and, finally, the Age of Louis XIV.
Voltaire sets forth quite clearly the standard by which he would
judge historical greatness: it is the cultural climax which comes
with the flowering of the arts and sciences. Why such a climax
came about in the ages he extolled he never satisfactorily explains; but he is absolutely certain that it occurred and was the
hallmark of greatness. In his present history he hopes to show
the extent of the cutural climax achieved during the age of
Louis XIV and how it surpassed all the others.

Originally Voltaire had set out to write a history of the arts
under Louis, but as he got deeper into his extensive research,
the work grew until it finally became part of a universal history
of mankind. The plan which he followed in presenting his material was not chronological but systematic; that is, he surveyed
the life of the time under its various aspects—political, economic,
moral, social, military, religious, scientific, and artistic—aiming in
this way at achieving a comprehensive and well-integrated picture
of a civilization. This plan has been criticized for its lack of unity,
coherence, and clarity, but it seems to have provided Voltaire
with the kind of framework he needed as he aspired "to provide
posterity with an account of the achievements of the human
spirit in the most enlightened age there has ever been." [31] He

realized that he had to be highly selective in what he included
and left out. "Not everything that has been done deserves to be
written about." [32] In *Louis XIV* he was concerned "only with
what merits the attention of all ages; with what depicts the
genius and the customs of men; and with whatever can serve
for instruction and recommend the love of virtue, of the arts
and of our country." [33] No one has described better the aesthetic
design of Voltaire's work than Gustave Lanson:

> The work unfolded on successive theatrical levels. After the grandiose
> proscenium depicting victories and conquests, there appeared the
> person of the king, the life and manners of the court, the refinement
> of the nobility, and the inner workings of the government, its useful
> institutions, and its ecclesiastical affairs. Finally, like a magnificent
> stage backdrop, there was the marvelous decor of arts, letters, and
> science, representing the outstanding achievement and superiority of
> seventeenth-century French civilization. The *Siècle* was planned and
> arranged as an apotheosis of the human spirit.[34]

Despite this magnificent plan which he labored to actualize
Voltaire never fully achieved his purpose in *The Age of Louis
XIV*. The background of the era remains shrouded in obscurity;
the nonchronological approach often defeats his aims as an historian; and the climax of the work and of the era—the all-
important account of the arts—is only sketched. As the historian
John B. Black points out, "in spite of the brilliance of the conception and the penetration displayed in the execution it remains
a torso." [35]

It is a tribute to Voltaire's skill as an artist-historian, though,
that his portrait of Louis XIV and his era has not faded more
with the passage of time and the accumulation of new facts and
interpretations, leaving a work retaining only antiquarian interest. *The Age of Louis XIV* remains vital and of perennial interest
to today's readers perhaps for the very reason that Voltaire
himself considered secondary: it gives an anecdotal history of a
fascinating ruler and his courtiers. Resolving not to resort to
anecdotes to ensure readership, Voltaire, a born *raconteur*, segre-
gated them in several central chapters of his work, which makes
them, and not the account of the arts, the heart of his work. The
king's majestic and awe-inspiring physical appearance is described.[36] His perfect poise, impeccable manners, and excellent

taste are illustrated. His gems of wisdom and penetrating insights into his courtiers are recorded. His personal charisma and private lusts, his fears and foibles, his delight in warfare and theatrical spectacle, in architecture and music, in painting and garden design—all are recorded for posterity's sake. All in all, Voltaire thinks that Louis merits the title "great." Despite his personal shortcomings—for example, his vanity, extravagance, and love of conflict—in Voltaire's view "Louis XIV did more for his people than twenty of his predecessors put together, and even then he did not do everything he might have done." [37] If today "Louis lives" it is to a considerable extent because Voltaire in his history caught him "warts and all."

In this part of the history one can observe Voltaire the dramatist and moralist at work, while Voltaire the historian dozes. Nowhere is this more apparent than in the description of the king's death.[38] This is presented in detail not only because Voltaire knew that his readers would be especially interested in how a man of such high estate is brought down to the most basic mortal level. It is also important in giving testimony to Voltaire's thesis that Louis was indeed a great man, not just because of his accomplishments in life but by his manner of confronting his own death. Contrasted with the death of his previous hero, Charles XII, which had been accidental, Voltaire's Louis XIV is depicted as meeting death in full consciousness and with moral determination to make his death, like his life, be of value to posterity. In a scene that well could have come from one of his own tragedies, Voltaire delivers the king's (and his) moral message. By this time the Sun King had long since passed the apogee of his long and eventful reign; his country faced ruin; and his personal happiness had recently been shattered by a series of deaths in his family. As he lay stricken on his deathbed at the age of seventy-seven, he said to his weeping wife (his former mistress Madame de Maintenon), "Why do you weep, did you think me immortal?" Later he managed to sit up in bed, took his soon-to-be-successor Louis XV in his arms and acknowledged his own errors as king, leaving him with the following advice:

Never . . . forget the obligation you are under to God . . . Endeavor to preserve peace with your neighbors . . . I have been too fond of war; in this do not follow my example any more than in my too expensive manner of living . . . Relieve your subjects as much as you can, and do what I have been so unhappy as not to be able to do myself.[39]

Another reason why *Louis XIV* retains its relevance and vitality as a classic in French and world literature is that it succeeded in capturing the essential features of one of the greatest cultural climaxes in history and one of the high points of Western civilization. As a contemporary historian recently pointed out, "Voltaire's position . . . remains valid, and the period in fact witnessed a genuine cultural climax." [40] Brief as they are, the chapters on the arts and sciences in *Louis XIV* tell us much of what we need to know about the intellectual life of an era in which, according to Voltaire, "mankind acquired throughout Europe greater light than in all the ages that preceded it." [41] It is this portion of Voltaire's history that forms its appropriate capstone as well as its justification.

But Voltaire wanted to do more in his work than to capture something of the grandeur of the Sun King's reign and to record for posterity the cultural climax in the arts and sciences which took place at the time, and thus made it one of the few great peaks in the history of civilization. He also wanted to inject his work into his own times by making it a vehicle for social criticism and an instrument to promote enlightenment. One way in which he did this indirectly was to hold up the ideal of greatness achieved under Louis XIV as a striking contrast to the mediocrity everywhere apparent under Louis XV. The fact that *The Age of Louis XIV*, upon publication, was seized and prohibited suggests strongly that its hidden message was recognized.

In later versions of his book, Voltaire saw to it that the social criticism and moral implications were made more explicit. Originally the chapters on the arts and sciences formed the climactic and concluding portions of the work. But in the 1760s, when Voltaire was a disillusioned courtier, a seasoned propagandist, and a militant opponent of religious fanaticism who would miss no opportunity to "crush the infamous thing," he added to *The Age of Louis XIV* several chapters on ecclesiastical affairs and conflicting religious groups of the time, including the Calvinists, Jansenists, and Quietists. A final chapter entitled "Disputes on Chinese Ceremonies" now brought the book to a close. Throughout his discussion of the religious quarrels Voltaire highlighted the incongruities of Christian doctrines, the foolish-ness of sectarian controversies, and the sufferings brought upon the innocent by religious bigotry, superstition, and fanaticism. The revocation of the Edict of Nantes by Louis in 1685, which led to renewed religious dissension and persecution—"a disgrace to human reason" in Voltaire's view—cast a dark shadow on a whole age, which otherwise was tending toward enlightenment.

"Disputes on Chinese Ceremonies," may at first sight seem an inappropriate and anticlimactic ending to an otherwise great work. The author would have been far wiser, some might argue, to have ended his history on the crescendo of cultural climax than on the rather cacophonous note of doctrinal dispute among Christians in an incongruous foreign setting. But upon closer reading it soon becomes apparent that "the sly old fox of Ferney" knew exactly what he was doing in giving his book on the grand *ancien régime* what is, in essence, a surprise ending. The surprise is that the chapter is really a kind of *conte,* a philosophical tale about a Chinese emperor who was far wiser in his ways than the warring factions from the West—the Dominican and Jesuit missionaries who became embroiled in a bitter quarrel over whether or not the Chinese were idolaters in their religious cere-monies and beliefs. Disenchanted with the quarrelsome priests who preached love while they practiced hate, the emperor "drove out all the missionaries and proscribed the Christian religion," restoring the peace, respect, and harmony characteristic of his venerable land.[42] Yon-tching, the emperor, is depicted as a Voltairian at heart; he has followed instinctively the motto: "*Ecrasez l'infâme!*" In this respect, he was far wiser, Voltaire seems to suggest, than his western counterpart Louis XIV who had allowed religious fanaticism to go unchecked, thus besmirch-ing an illustrious era and repressing the development of the critical, philosophical consciousness. "Disputes on Chinese Cere-monies" illustrates very well the increasingly important role that the aged Voltaire was performing as historian-philosopher, that of promoting tolerance, reason, and brotherhood.

Thus Voltaire brings down the curtain on *The Age of Louis XIV* by striking a new and controversial note thirty years after the work was first conceived. Though it is a flawed masterpiece, it is still eminently readable and worth reading. "*The Age of Louis XIV,*" wrote the French philosopher, the Marquis de Con-dorcet, "is the only history of that reign that one has to read." [43]

It continues to attract attention today by its twofold appeal: it is a monument to a great age of creativity by a great creative spirit.

VI   A *Universal View of History:* Essay on Customs *(1756)*

Voltaire's *Essay on the Customs and the Spirit of Nations* might have been better entitled *An Enlightened Man's View of the Past and Hope for the Future.* It is more a philosophy of history than a history, strictly speaking. It contains much of what we would today call anthropology, sociology, and psychology. It is supposedly objective and comprehensive in its approach to history, but contains a good deal of moralizing about the past as well as, according to some of its critics, a certain amount of special pleading. One of these critics, Voltaire's great contemporary Montesquieu, claimed that "Voltaire is like the monks who write not for the sake of the subject they treat, but for the glory of their order; he writes for the convent." [44] From this point of view, then, Voltaire, *philosophe par excellence,* was viewing and writing history for his fellow would-be enlighteners. He was performing a task in the eighteenth century that H. G. Wells performed for the twentieth; his *Essay* is an *Outline of History* for reformers.

Originally, Voltaire had conceived the project of writing a new kind of universal history when his blue-stocking mistress Madame du Châtelet had complained of the tediousness and irrelevance of most history books. Why should she have to be burdened with "a confused mass of unrelated facts, a thousand accounts of battles which have decided nothing?" [45] Far better to devote one's time to the clarity and concreteness of science and mathematics than to the obscurity and specificity of history. Voltaire was convinced that, while Emilie was right about previous histories, he—poet, dramatist, and already experienced historian—could meet her challenge. He would prove to her that history didn't have to be boring; that readers didn't have to be buried in piles of facts in order to be informed about what happened of genuine significance in the past; and that the whole historical process could be made to unfold in its own fascinating manner without bringing in "divine destiny" or focusing on a "chosen people," as the pious Bishop Bossuet had done in his supposedly universal history. The important thing was to stick to essentials; not to try to tell all, but to tell all that was necessary. That, and only that, would be enough.

This greatest of all Voltaire's historical works was, then, from one point of view, a labor of love intended to meet the challenge of a lover. Through three decades he continued to work on it, publishing a portion of it in 1745, the definitive text in 1756, and a final version, which brought the work right up into the time of Louis XV, in 1763. Along with the *Encyclopedia,* it became one of the essential books which every well-educated man and woman of the time knew or at least knew of. Voltaire's fellow *philosophes* extolled it. Even an empress, Catherine the Great of Russia, wrote Voltaire that if she had any knowledge she owed it to him, and that she would like to learn every page of his *Essay* by heart.[46] His original ideal for a truly interesting history book for Emilie had succeeded beyond his wildest dreams. History, he had shown, could be popularized and still be history. Or was it history after all? "The *Essai sur les Moeurs,*" writes a recent historian, "is one of the strangest books ever written by an historian." [47]

Voltaire's history, as he originally envisaged it, would begin when the Archbishop Bossuet's history had ended—with the reign of Charlemagne. But, in fact, after a long and rambling philosophical introduction he began it in ancient China. This undoubtedly made sense to Voltaire as he made clear that, from the start, his history, unlike Bossuet's, would be truly catholic (i.e., universal). He was including in the historical pageant not only the aspirations and achievements of the West, but those of all people from China to America, from India to Africa. In this way, he hoped to avoid the myopia of nationalistic, ethnic, and religious biases, and would write history not as a Frenchman but as a philosopher. And to be a philosopher, in his opinion, meant maintaining an impartial, universal, reflective, and sceptical frame of mind.

Today Voltaire's commencement of his historical account with China does not seem strange at all; in fact, despite his limited knowledge of the dynastic development of China, what he says about the contributions of the Middle Kingdom to world civilization makes good sense, and must endear him to contemporary Sinophiles. His motives in praising the Chinese were not, however, totally disinterested. In his seemingly detached way he was criticizing, by implication, certain aspects of Western Judeo-Christian tradition that he found highly objectionable. We have already seen him doing this in the final chapter on "Disputes on Chinese Ceremonies" of *The Age of Louis XIV*. Sometimes it even seems that his antipathy to Christianity is so strong that he is inclined to praise some religious beliefs and practices in other cultures simply because they are not Christian. Usually, however, he gives reasons for preferring one way of life over another; for example, he considers the Chinese to be more civilized than other so-called civilized people because they are the only people who never practiced sacrificing children to propitiate gods. Above all, he commends the Chinese for their morals and laws which, in his opinion, are certainly on a par with Western ones, if not superior.[48] Confucius, as a moralist and sage, deserves a place of honor along with Jesus and Socrates. Not surprisingly, the sage of Ferney finds much to identify with in the Chinese teacher's rationality, humanism, and common sense.

Leaving Confucian China, Voltaire traces the development of the Islamic cultures of the Middle East before he turns his attention finally to the Christian West which, he now has made clear, is only a part and not even necessarily the preeminent part, of the whole historical panorama. The prophet Mohammed, who had already been the subject of one of Voltaire's most successful and controversial tragedies, is treated here supposedly not with the imagination of a dramatist but with the objectivity of an historian. Yet here, as in *Mohammed*, the prophet is the paradigm of the religious fanatic. In a passage that suggests the ideological concerns that sometimes blinded Voltaire's view of history, he writes:

It is probable that Mohammed, like all enthusiasts, being forcibly struck with his own ideas, uttered them at first as he felt them; these growing afterwards more strong by being repeated, he deceived himself while he was deceiving others; and at length he had recourse to imposture to support a doctrine which he thought right.[49]

Proceeding to the West, Voltaire begins by arguing (as Edward Gibbon would later agree) that Christianity, after the decline and fall of the Roman empire, achieved its success not by promoting but by abandoning its religious ideals. Charlemagne, the founder of the Holy Roman Empire, is, in Voltaire's opinion, "one

of the strongest proofs that success sanctifies injustice, and con-
quers glory. . . . This man, who shed such a torrent of blood,
robbed his nephews of their patrimony, and was suspected of
incest, has, by the Church of Rome, been ranked among the
number of saints." [50] Having passed this judgment on the man
whom many considered to be the father of European civilization,
Voltaire continues to trace the development of the various European nations—France, Spain, England, Austria, Russia, and the
rest—after the breakdown of Charlemagne's empire. Seldom does
he lose sight of his goal—to focus on "the customs, manners and
spirit of the principal nations" as he recounts lucidly the lengthy
and complicated stages through which modern Western civilization reached its high mark in seventeenth-century France.

Although he tries to be objective about the papacy and recognizes some of the contributions the Church made in the Middle
Ages, Voltaire's hatred of institutionalized Christianity is never
far from the surface in his account of the Crusades, the Protestant
Reformation, and the Catholic Counter-Reformation. "The history
of the great events of this world," he writes, "is scarcely anything
but a detail of crimes. I do not find any age which the ambition
of the laity and the clergy has not filled with horrors." [51] At another point in his narrative he comments: "In all the disputes
which have armed the Christians against each other, since the
first rise of their Church, the See of Rome has always sided with
that doctrine which tended the most to degrade human understanding, and obscure the light of reason." [52] Humanity, he believes, would still be "in a state little better than that of savage
beasts" had it not produced at least a few extraordinary persons
such as the English king Alfred the Great whom because of his
moderation, his love of learning, his mild laws, and his liberality,
Voltaire places "in the first rank of those heroes who have been
of service to mankind." [53] Henry IV of France, whom Voltaire
had already praised in his *Henriade,* is also singled out as a
public benefactor for his bravery, honesty, mercifulness, and
spirit of toleration.[54] Thus, in Voltaire's vision of the drama of
history, Eastern as well as Western, the personified forces of
knowledge, morality, and science are always pitted against those
of ignorance, human depravity, and religious superstition. "Human nature is never so debased as when ignorance is armed with
power." In the light of such beliefs, history, to Voltaire as to
H. G. Wells, is always a race between education and catastrophe.

In his "Recapitulation" to his panoramic survey Voltaire seems to take a tragic view of history. The countless series of revolutions which the world has experienced since the time of Charlemagne, he says, have only tended "to desolation, and the loss of millions of lives." [55] Great events have been capital misfortunes. History recounts not times of peace and tranquility, but only "ravages and disasters." "All history, in short," he states, "is little else than a long succession of useless cruelties, . . . a collection of crimes, follies, and misfortunes, among which we have now and then met with a few virtues, and some happy times, as we see sometimes a few scattered huts in a barren desert." [56] The cause of this, he goes on to point out, lies in the heart of man, in his pride and arrogance, his cruelty and fanaticism. From man, not from God, springs the historical record that is "almost a succession of crimes and disasters." [57]

Yet Voltaire's final conclusion to his history is not pessimistic. He retains hope that history will not always be a record of catastrophes, and maintains his faith in man as he may someday become in a more civilized, humanized, and enlightened age. The humanistic, philosophical spirit is working its way in history to transform the world through "its gradually expanding light." This is Voltaire's conclusion:

Finally, one cannot but believe that reason and human industry will continue to make further progress; that the useful arts will be developed; that prejudices, which are not the least of the many scourges which afflict mankind, will gradually disappear among all the leaders of nations, and that philosophy, widespread through the world, will go some way toward consoling human nature for the calamities which it will suffer in every age.[58]

This passage could well have served as a preface for Condorcet's later *Sketch of the Progress of the Human Mind*. It certainly supports a recent commentator's view that "Voltaire was primarily a moralist chiefly concerned with spreading the gospel of enlightenment," which taught that humanity could be saved by reason rather than by faith, philosophy rather than religion, and peaceful industry rather than warfare.[59] Voltaire himself viewed his vocation as an historian in this way. Of his *Essay* he said: "Humanity dictated it and Truth held the pen." [60]

Today Voltaire's attempt at a universal history may seem

extremely sketchy, incoherent, and naive. Its moralistic under-tones distract many readers while its antireligious asides offend others. Its author's rationalistic assumptions blinded him to many important components in the historical process. As two recent American historians point out, Voltaire was "so much a victim of the 18th century's inability to conceive of men as different—of, as [Arthur] Lovejoy puts it, its 'uniformitarian' view of human nature—that he made deists out of the Chinese and natural philosophers out of the American Indians." [61] But, as the French historian Jules Michelet long ago recognized, it is "this History which made all historiography, which begot all of us, critics and narrators alike." [62]

CHAPTER 4

The Eye of Eighteenth Century Illumination: Voltaire as Philosopher

VOLTAIRE has often been called a propagandist rather than a philosopher, a committed polemicist rather than a critical and impartial examiner of ideas. He himself never claimed to be a professional philosopher; but he did claim to be a proponent of philosophy in the sense in which he defined it—"enlightened love of wisdom, sustained by love of God."[1] His sceptical and critical spirit, his conviction that ideas matter in the world of affairs, and his synoptic method were characteristic of his role as philosopher. He was not an originator of ideas, but an expositor and popularizer of them. While the theory of the universe that he accepted was not of his own making, he expounded it, promulgated it, and defended it ably and at times brilliantly. Like other philosophers however, he had human biases which sometimes interfered with the open-mindedness, flexibility, and rational judgment he valued and usually manifested.

Voltaire's reading of philosophical works was amazingly extensive and varied, and his intellectual and intuitive understanding of the meaning and implications of ideas was remarkable for a nonprofessional. He remained throughout his life an amateur compared with the true professionals—Descartes, Locke, Spinoza, Leibniz, and others—from whom he drew inspiration and sustenance. But so well did he absorb, synthesize, and utilize the impressions which he garnered from others and from his own experience, that this highly talented "amateur," this poet-turned-philosopher, eventually produced not just a "chaos of clear ideas" but a reasonably coherent universe of relevant concepts by which revolutionary changes could be brought about in the world. Voltaire was, in the words of John Morley, "the eye of eighteenth century illumination."[2]

Voltaire was not alone, of course, in trying to apply philosophy to change the world. He was one of the birds-of-a-feather called *philosophes,* a circle of critical free-thinkers who, while differing considerably among themselves, shared in common the ideal of enlightenment. As Immanuel Kant formulated it, this ideal could be summed up in the admonition: "Dare to know! Have the courage to use your own intelligence!"[3] Albert Guérard defined a *philosophe* as "essentially a critic of abuses and a promoter of reforms."[4] In France the main *philosophes* were Voltaire, Diderot, D'Alembert, and Baron d'Holbach. In Germany, Immanuel Kant; in England, Adam Smith; and in America, Benjamin Franklin were representative *philosophes.* "The main tenets of the group," writes Norman L. Torrey in *Les Philosophes,* "[were] a firm belief in the idea of progress, the application of the experimental method in science, the free and unfettered use of the God-given faculty of reason in all affairs, human and divine, and the ardent faith that reason, with all its limitations, was the final judge and the best guide available for the conduct of life."[5]

In developing and defending these ideas, the *philosophes* drew heavily on English empirical and liberal philosophers. "They were trinitarians," Peter Gay remarks, "and their trinity consisted of Bacon, Newton, and Locke."[6] Certainly in this respect Voltaire was *philosophe par excellence.* For it was in England that he first encountered the kind of faith in science, the hope that reason would prevail, and the love of freedom that gave him a philosophical platform from which to survey his own country's faults and to foresee the remedies that would have to be applied to correct these faults. *Philosophical Letters,* his first philosophical work, is a monument to Voltaire's Anglophilia.

While the *Philosophical Letters* and the *Philosophical Dictionary* are representative and important expressions of Voltaire's philosophy, such works are by no means the only expressions of it. Many of his plays, *contes,* poems, dialogues, essays, and letters manifest his philosophical concerns, and often set forth the same or similar ideas which are developed more rigorously and in greater detail in his major discursive philosophical works. *Candide* fictionalizes the problem of evil which is discussed earlier in the *Poem on the Lisbon Disaster* and later in the *Philosophical Dictionary.* Fate is a concept dealt with not only in *Zadig* but also in the *Treatise on Metaphysics.* Self-love is a topic in both *Dis-*

courses in Verse on Man and *The Ignorant Philosopher.* And so
on. Practically everything Voltaire wrote is permeated with his
scepticism, his hostility toward organized religion, his deism, and
his humanistic values. Voltaire's philosophy is expressed in his
works, and in every one of them.

I   *Liberating Ideas:* Philosophical Letters *(1734)*

Lytton Strachey may have exaggerated the importance of
Voltaire's visit to England when he claimed that it "marks a
turning-point in the history of civilization," but he correctly ap-
praised the book that came out of that visit, the *Philosophical
Letters,* as "a fulcrum by means of which the lever of Voltaire's
philosophy is brought into operation." [7] When the *Letters* appeared in Voltaire's native country, the book was promptly
recognized for what it was intended to be—an all-out attack on
the French establishment, an indirect but dangerous attempt to
undermine the religious, political, and philosophical foundations
of institutions that had long been considered sacrosanct. It was
as though the recently returned poet was waving a flag of
liberation in the face of a repressive and arrogant regime. No
wonder it was immediately seized and given a public burning;
no wonder its author was described as an enemy of the state.
The book may have been philosophical to Voltaire, but it was
incendiary to its critics.

What is philosophical about the *Philosophical Letters?* First
of all, they reflect clearly the author's probing, inquisitive mind.
He is curious about his subject matter, a unique and interesting
people—the English—and as he proceeds in his attempt to comprehend and clarify to himself their *esprit,* their behavior and
accomplishments, he imparts to his readers his own sense of
wonderment at the novel and diverting human spectacle called
England. Sometimes, like a visitor from another planet, he seems
to assume a detached and disinterested perspective; he is struck
by the strangeness of the rare and mysterious earthlings. Sometimes he is delighted and amused by their behavior. If he is ever
offended or disgusted by it he does not admit it. His attitude
throughout the book is that of a man who has "waked up to
wonder," which is exactly one definition of a philosopher.

Voltaire's discussion of the English philosophers—John Locke
(Letter XIII), Francis Bacon (Letter XII), and Sir Isaac New-

ton—suggests another related philosophical aspect of his *Letters,*
their sceptical, free-thinking, and even subversive orientation.
For Voltaire, as for Albert Camus, to think is to undermine.
Francis Bacon, as the father of experimental philosophy, had
undermined speculative metaphysics and awakened man's
consciousness to the feats that could be accomplished by his
unhampered creative intellect. Sir Isaac Newton had completed
the demolition of the old Ptolemaic view of the universe, re-
placing it with a rational and scientifically verifiable theory. For
many years to come Voltaire was to study and to promote
Newton's ideas. He felt that Newton's and Locke's ideas were
especially needed in France as a sensible replacement of Cartesian
misconceptions. In Voltaire's view, Descartes' concept of man
and the universe was an "ingenious romance" compared with
that of Newton and Locke.[8] A man could not be a true philosopher and accept the French philosopher's outmoded, *a priori*
basis of thought, he claimed.

Much as he admired Bacon and Newton, Voltaire's favorite
English philosopher was John Locke, whom he praised on every
possible occasion. Starting from the radical and common-sensical
assumption that there can be no knowledge without sense impressions, Locke had shown that the ideas accepted by the
majority of metaphysicians were completely without foundation.
What sensations can one present to prove the existence of an
underlying "incorporeal essence," supposedly referred to by the
word "soul"? If there is nothing in the understanding that has
not come into it through sense impressions, what evidence is
there for believing in innate ideas? Who needs them or wants
them if they can be shown to be superfluous metaphysical bag-
gage? Voltaire himself speaks with all the fervor of a new convert
to Locke's empiricism.[9] What we experience, he argues, are sensations and ideas of sensations which, as Locke showed so
patiently and exhaustively in his *Essay concerning Human Understanding,* are built up into the complex structure of knowledge
through association and recollection. The mind is not some sort
of theoretical machinery which produces knowledge through its
own internal operations; it is a *tabula rasa,* a blank tablet, which
would always remain blank did not the pen of experience write
upon it.

Such a view of knowledge, Voltaire recognized, can have
devastating repercussions on dogmatic theologians who persist

in the false belief that the existence of an immortal soul is a logically provable dogma. An empirical and scientific approach to knowledge is not, however, necessarily antireligious or atheistic. It simply refuses to probe into the mysteries of religious beliefs, but is willing to leave them as articles of faith within a separate higher domain. Locke certainly believed in God. There was plenty of room in Newton's universe for God and for theology, but he kept them separate from his interest in natural philosophy. Voltaire's own belief in God remained unshaken as he immersed his thinking in British empiricism. A few years after his return to France, nevertheless, he did feel compelled to take a new "inventory of his beliefs" (as Professor Wade puts it) in his *Treatise on Metaphysics* which includes arguments for the existence of God.[10]

Religion, always one of Voltaire's strongest philosophical concerns, is the subject of four of his *Philosophical Letters*, though the subject is discussed not abstractly but through the description of a then-new English sect, the Quakers. On the surface Voltaire appears to be mainly interested in the novel beliefs and eccentric behavior of the Society of Friends. Using as a vehicle an interview with a kind old Quaker, the narrator delights in presenting an image of the sect's unique dress, manners, language, worship services, and doctrines.[11] But underlying all this, is the author's interest in freedom of inquiry and tolerance of religious and philosophical diversity of belief. If at times he seems to be satirizing the Quakers, he is more often pointing out characteristics of their beliefs and practices that he finds commendable. The gentle, loving spirit of the Quakers, their rejection of an elaborate theology and a priestly caste, their independence of judgment and their moral courage and honesty, their pacifism, their insistence on liberty of conscience, and, above all, their practice of religious tolerance—these were features that Voltaire greatly admired in them and found sadly lacking in the religious behavior of his fellow Frenchmen, to whom his *Philosophical Letters* were addressed. And the image of the kindly Quaker, a perfect deist, lingered with Voltaire throughout his life. We shall meet him again in the *Philosophical Dictionary* and in *The Story of Johnny*, one of Voltaire's last *contes*, written about forty years after his *Philosophical Letters*.

From his account of the various sects—the Quakers, the Anglicans, the Presbyterians, and the Unitarians—which he

singled out for discussion, Voltaire drew an important conclusion
about the relationship between religious diversity and toleration:

If one religion only were allowed in England, the government would
very possibly become arbitrary; if there were but two, the people
would cut one another's throats; but, as there is such a multitude,
they all live happily, and in peace.[12]

As a practicing poet and dramatist Voltaire was especially
interested in getting acquainted with English literature and
theater. Jonathan Swift, who was later to have a strong influence
on his satirical works, he considered to be "Rabelais in his right
senses, but polished by frequenting the best company." [13]
Alexander Pope, a kindred spirit in didactic poetry, was "the most
harmonious poet that England has hitherto produced" who "has
reduced the shrill harshness of the English trumpet to the soft
sweetness of the Lydian flute." [14] Of the previous English writers
he singled out for praise especially John Milton, Samuel Butler,
John Dryden, and—with some reservation—William Shakespeare.
Shakespeare was an astonishing phenomenon which challenged
and perplexed him. What could he, a dedicated neoclassicist,
make of a genius "at once strong and abundant, natural and
sublime, but without the smallest spark of taste, and void of the
remotest idea of the rules"? [15] While judging him to be "rude and
unpolished" he could not help but admire and praise Shakespeare
for infusing a strength and energy into the English language
which has never been surpassed. He tried to cut Shakespeare's
genius as a dramatist down to size so that he could comprehend
it. The Elizabethan had drawn his characters and plots from
older histories and romances; he pandered to the interest of his
audiences by including in his plays "everything that can please
the curious"; "a few strokes of genius, a few happy lines replete
with nature and force" had eventually turned admiration for
Shakespeare into idolization, raising his reputation to the point
where some Englishmen considered him "another Sophocles."
The example of Shakespeare's success, nevertheless, convinced
Voltaire not only of the diversity of tastes among nations, but
also that there were ways of achieving the highest dramatic
effects without rigidly adhering to the traditional and accepted
Aristotelian canons. After Shakespeare, drama—including Voltaire's—would never be the same. He would never renounce his

neoclassical ideals and practices to become as free as Shakespeare; but he would draw ideas from the great English dramatist when the need arose, and it did, for example, in *Zaïre,* which showed the influence of *Othello.*

Yet Voltaire was so puzzled by the excesses of English tragedy that it sometimes seemed "as if nature were not the same in England as elsewhere." [16] He considered the English taste for buffoonery, especially mixed into tragedy, excessive and offensive. He found it impossible to reconcile "so much good sense with such absurdity, so much meanness with such sublimity of expression." He compared the English poetical genius to a luxuriant unshaped tree which would die if it were cropped and trained in a manner fit for a formal French garden. Nevertheless, he admired the naturalness, the boldness, and profundity of the English language, which in English tragedy and comedy revealed its uniqueness and power. The English poet, in his view, was a free man who could subject his language to his genius. His French counterpart, on the other hand, was always expected to conform to the rules of poetry and remain a slave to rhyme. As he put it later, "an Englishman says what he will; a Frenchman only what he can." [17]

But aesthetic restraints were not the only restraints that bothered Voltaire as he reflected on the differences between England and France. From one point of view, his *Philosophical Letters* can be viewed as "a poet's revenge" against the injustices he has suffered at the hands of his fellow countrymen. From the safe and sane vantage point of a liberal foreign country, he had come to realize that such things should not have been allowed to happen. He had twice been imprisoned for his writings; the king had refused to allow him to dedicate his national epic poem to him; his noble friends had scoffed at the idea of supporting him after he had been beaten at the instigation of one of their fellow noblemen. He had had to go into exile to avoid being further hounded by the French police. How bleak seemed the life of the artist in France contrasted with his life in England! It was as though France still suffered from a bad conscience passed down from its medieval Christian heritage, with its sense of original sin. Artists were considered mere entertainers and not entrusted, as in England, with government positions. Writers were viewed as subversives because they encouraged people to think for themselves and not to accept authority unquestioningly. All of this bitterness and long-suppressed rage surfaced in his *Philosophical Letters,* disguised by sparkling wit and rendered more palatable by a lucid and captivating style.

The twenty-third letter "On the Consideration Owed to Men of Letters" expresses most directly Voltaire's personal feelings on the subject of the relationship of the artist to society. It begins with an embrace and ends with a slap in the face. "Neither in England nor in any other country in the world does one find such establishments for the sake of the fine arts as there are in France." [18] But shortly after this flattering reference to French cultural institutions, Voltaire is lashing his country for not showing more respect and recognition for its artists, writers, and scientists. In France, he comments ironically, a dramatist such as Joseph Addison, if he had been lucky, might have belonged to an academy or won a pension through the influence of some woman or, if he had been unlucky, might have been imprisoned on the pretext that some lines of his were directed against a powerful man. In England, however, Addison was secretary of state. The greatest English geniuses—Newton, Congreve, Prior, Swift—had been elevated to positions of power and prestige or at least had won fortunes and recognition. How sorry would have been their plight in France! Voltaire delivers a venomous sting by reminding Frenchmen of how some of their most distinguished authors, such as Prosper Jolyot de Crébillon and Louis Racine, had been reduced practically to starvation. And he does not let them forget either that they allowed the body of one of the greatest French actresses, Adrienne Lecouvreur, to be thrown into a lime pit. In England she would have had the national honor of a burial in Westminster Abbey! The letter ends in a tirade against the "gothic barbarity that some dare to call Christian severity" of those who have condemned actors in France as impious and have censored works of dramatic geniuses.

Throughout his discussion of the arts and sciences in England, Voltaire points out the vital relationship between the health of the aesthetic, literary, and scientific life of a society and the health of its body politic. If in England thinking is more valued, learning more honored, artistic creation and performance more appreciated and respected, and artists and scientists better rewarded than in France, it is not an accident. Nor is it due to the fact that English people are by nature superior to French people. The chief reason is that the English have a different and better form of government. And this leads to a final aspect of Voltaire's *Letters* which is philosophical—the social and the political perspective expressed in them.

In two letters "On the Parliament" and "On Government" Voltaire gives a brief account of the British political system and its differences from the French. The key passage in his whole discussion and the one in which he transmits his message most explicitly to his readers is this:

The English are the only people on earth who have been able to prescribe limits to the power of kings by resisting them, and who, by a series of struggles, have at length established that wise and happy form of government where the prince is all-powerful to do good, and at the same time is restrained from committing evil; where the nobles are great without insolence or lordly power, and the people share in the government without confusion.[19]

Voltaire's description of the British system is succinct and penetrating. He refers to the House of Lords and the House of Commons as "the arbiters of the nation," and to the king as "the umpire."[20] He admires the balance of power which has been thus achieved. Internal discord and social injustice seem to him to be reduced to the minimum through the unwritten, but ever-evolving English constitution. The spirit of the laws seems to be omnipresent and omnipotent. Furthermore, the system's openness, flexibility, and freedom have made the English not only jealous guardians of their own liberty, but also supporters of the liberty of others. A study of English history reveals that the price for establishing the English system of government has been paid in blood, but Voltaire believes it was well worth it. At least in England civil war had not ended in slavery, as it often had in other countries, but in freedom.

The picture of England that emerges from Voltaire's *Philosophical Letters* is intentionally utopian. England, unlike France, is envisaged as a true land of freedom: freedom of thought, freedom of action, freedom of creation—all of these rested upon political freedom. Voltaire knew that he was exaggerating, of course. But he wanted to make sure that his message did not go unnoticed by those who otherwise might be apt to ignore it.

II *In Defense of Man: Voltaire versus Pascal*

The last of Voltaire's *Philosophical Letters,* and the most strictly philosophical of all, is number twenty-five entitled "On the *Thoughts* of M. Pascal." Why was this included in a collection of letters dealing with philosophical reflections on England? Does it have any relationship to what has preceded or was it added as an afterthought? Even though some French commentators on the *Letters* see this last one as a philosophical outcome of the lessons Voltaire had learned in England, its content is such that it has no obvious relationship to the other letters, except in its critical tone. Yet a unity is achieved, for the *Letters* began with a discussion of religion—Quakerism—and, now, with the inclusion of the debate with Pascal—ended with one. It was this latter discussion, in fact, which the French authorities found one of the most objectionable features of the book. In attacking Blaise Pascal, Voltaire could be considered to be attacking Jansenism, a religious force which still dominated the French *parlements.*

Whatever his reasons for including the essay on Pascal in the French edition of his *Letters,* he makes it quite clear that his main objection to Pascal's views was the latter's insistence on showing mankind "in an odious light." This seventeenth-century ascetic genius was "dead set on depicting us all as wicked and wretched." Consequently, he wrote "against the human race in much the same strain as he wrote against the Jesuits." Voltaire intends to show that Pascal's views on human nature are prejudiced, distorted, pessimistic, and irrational. "I shall be so bold," he declares, "as to defend my fellow creatures against the invectives of this sublime misanthrope." Voltaire will show that "we are neither so wretched nor so wicked as he declares us to be." [21]

Voltaire's method of attack is to set forth a number of Pascal's *Pensées* and, following a good scholastic procedure, to state his objections to them. For example, Pascal claimed that only the Christian religion could explain the contradictions in human nature. Voltaire objects that there is no reason why such contradictions cannot be explained and resolved by alternative religions and philosophies. Christianity, in his view, has no monopoly on psychological understanding. Further, Pascal considers man to be a mysterious creature, an enigma that is inconceivable without accepting the doctrines of Christian faith which are based on original sin. Voltaire objects that the human predicament can be understood without viewing it as enigmatic. Man, in his view, is a natural creature in a natural world, an animal (although superior) among other animals. Human existence includes good and evil, pleasure and pain. It is sometimes puzzling and painful, but it is not inherently mysterious or tragic.

As he continues in this way to refute Pascal's views on man, Voltaire's confirmed optimism becomes apparent. He does not believe with Pascal that men are doomed to a life of misery, conflict, and unhappiness. "To consider the universe as a dreary dungeon, and all mankind as so many condemned wretches being carried to execution, is the idea of a mad fanatic." [22] Through human efforts problems can be solved, miseries removed, conflicts resolved.

Voltaire also takes Pascal to task for claiming that self-love is sinful and evil. To the contrary, self-love, as Voltaire sees it, is a healthy instinct, implanted in us by God so that we can meet our own needs and the needs of others. Without the continuing operation of self-love, regulated by law and perfected by religion, civilization itself would never have come about. Nor is he willing to accept Pascal's view that self-introspection inevitably fills one with fear and loathing. Voltaire has no sympathy for those who claim they are experiencing what existentialists today call an "existential vacuum." His answer to any such gloomy thoughts is, in a word, action. "Man is born for action as the fire tends upwards, and a stone downwards." [23] Yet in the very process of rejecting the feelings that today we would call existentialist, Voltaire reaches a kind of existentialist affirmation. "Not to be occupied, and not to exist, is one and the same thing with regard to man." [24] We should act in order to ameliorate the human condition, Voltaire holds, not waste our time brooding about it.

Believing as he does that God's existence can be proven by reason and experience (at least with a high degree of probability), Voltaire sees no value in Pascal's agonizing over conflicting arguments, his proposal to wager that God exists, and his reliance, ultimately, upon faith and revelation.

Such is the drift of Voltaire's attempt to "refute" Pascal—or "Blaise Condor," as he sometimes later called him. [25] He felt he must dispel Pascal's spirit—the spirit of the fanatical believer—in order to clear the way for optimistic deism. He admired the famous Jansenist's vision and style, but rejected what to him seemed a slanderous attack on mankind.

III *Theoretical Underpinnings:* Treatise on Metaphysics *(1734)*

Voltaire's *Philosophical Letters* reflected the ferment of ideas incited by his English sojourn. While they were not intended as a statement of a coherent world view, they marked an important stage along the way toward his developing a philosophy to live by. Locke's empiricism had especially stimulated Voltaire to further hard thinking. What he needed now was a chance to formulate and to grapple with the fundamental problems of human existence. If one followed Locke's empirical direction, which seemed to Voltaire the correct way, could one still find grounds for believing in God and the soul? Could one explain the relationship between thinking and material existence? Could one find a basis for morality that was not purely relative and arbitrary? In this metaphysical and ethical search Madame du Châtelet gave Voltaire great encouragement, and the result of his inquiries, the little treatise on metaphysics which was never published during his lifetime, was lovingly dedicated to her.[26]

The whole approach of Voltaire in this treatise is humanistic. Metaphysics is worth studying, he believes, only if it has some direct relationship and relevance to human beings—to their doubts, to their self-understanding, and to their relationship with one another. As pure theory metaphysics might be fascinating, like pure mathematics, but Voltaire wanted more than intellectual satisfaction from theorizing. He wanted answers which would teach him and others how to live better and more enlightened lives. Later, Voltaire was often to speak of metaphysics as a waste of time, perhaps because he had already found his own answers to metaphysical questions; but in this early stage of his philosophical development he is still open-minded. He is not yet the scoffer of whom it was later said that he despised the metaphysical questions as much as their supposed solutions. In fact, his little treatise is perhaps the most abstract, the most purely theoretical, and the most tightly reasoned of all the works he ever wrote. At the time it seemed to him to be the most practical and human.

The first question Voltaire considers in his treatise is whether or not there is a God. He never seems to have seriously doubted His existence, but he clearly states the pros and cons of the argument. One could not ask for a clearer, more succinct statement of the metaphysical arguments both for and against belief in a deity. Voltaire shows that, when he wants to, he can write textbook metaphysics in which his old Jesuit teachers might well have taken pride. His first argument, which to him seems "the most natural and the most perfect," considers "not only the order which is in the universe, but the end to which each thing appears to be related." [27]

When I see a watch whose hands mark the hours, I conclude that an intelligent being has arranged the springs of this machine, so that the hands mark the hours. Thus, when I see the springs of the human body, I conclude that an intelligent being has arranged these organs in order that they may be received and nourished nine months in the womb; that the eyes are given for seeing, the hands for grasping, etc.[28]

This is plausible enough. Voltaire is careful to point out, however, that no one has yet discovered anything about the ultimate nature of this higher intelligent being.

The second argument, which seems "more metaphysical" to Voltaire, starts from the fact that "I exist, therefore something exists." Without restating the argument in detail here, it can be summed up as the old scholastic argument (which St. Thomas Aquinas had derived from Aristotle) which hinges on the distinction between contingent (i.e., dependent) and necessary being. If we do not assume that there is an ultimate necessary being which accounts for the existence of all contingent (i.e., intermediary) beings, we cannot explain why they are at all; that is, why there is something rather than nothing. To suppose that an existing being has the source of its being in another being, which in turn owes its existence to a third being, and so on *ad infinitum*, is absurd, since no being would ever have an ultimate source of existence. Therefore, one must conclude that an ultimate and necessary being, the ground of all contingent being, exists, and this we call God.

Here we cannot follow Voltaire as he weaves his way through the intricacies of metaphysical arguments for and against the existence of God. They are not original by any means, but derived from earlier sources, from John Locke, Samuel Clarke, and the French rationalists. It is important to note, however, that he gives equal space to the objections to God's existence as to the arguments for it.[29] Among the most important of these are the arguments from the pessimistic view that there is evidence of imperfections in the design of things which cannot be reconciled with belief in God, and the materialist view that one is justified in assuming that nature, not God, is the ultimate eternal and infinite being. The thrust of Voltaire's answers to these objections is to insist that a universally binding cosmic order is far to be preferred to an arbitrary scheme, even if at the human level there may be apparent contradictions, which lead to suffering and perplexity. Further, he points out that our attempt to understand the purpose of things is often vitiated by our own narrow perspective, self-centeredness, and ignorance.

Having established, at least in his own mind, that the existence of God, if not absolutely certain, is at least highly probable, Voltaire turns to the discussion of other metaphysical questions.[30] He proceeds to explain, closely following Locke, how all of our ideas are derived from sense impressions. He then tackles the exceedingly difficult problem of the relationship between thought and material or bodily manifestations, a question which had perplexed both rationalists and materialists before him. He considers the possible existence and nonexistence of a soul and, like Locke, remains sceptical that the reality of any sort of "incorporeal essence," or underlying spiritual substance, can be proven if one starts from empiricist assumptions. He is unwilling to suppose, therefore, that that which is called soul is immortal.

One of the most interesting sections of the *Treatise* is devoted to whether man is free, a topic on which Voltaire had engaged in correspondence with Frederick the Great. Here Voltaire argues for at least limited freedom. "The liberty given by God to man is the feeble power, limited and transitory, of applying to oneself certain thoughts and of operating certain movements." [31] Later in life he was to change his mind on this crucial issue, and to argue, for the most part as a determinist, that the course of events is inexorably determined by natural law and cannot be interrupted by human or even by divine intervention.

The last two chapters of the *Treatise* are concerned with ques-

tions which, strictly speaking, are ethical rather than metaphysical. Some scholars believe these chapters were added to the
treatise after it was finished in response to criticism and discussion, and upon further reflection. The English deist Bernard
Mandeville is the inspiration here rather than Locke. Voltaire
argues that man is by nature not a selfish animal, but capable of
disinterested or unselfish actions, motivated by sympathy and
kindness toward his fellow creatures. Although he rejects the
notion that there is any sort of supernatural sanction for morality,
this does not lead him to defend a moral relativism according to
which morals are simply matters of mores in different cultures.
"Virtue and vice, the good and the morally bad, is . . . in all
countries that which is useful or useless to the society." [32] In all
places and at all times, he adds, "the one who sacrifices most to
the public is the one who is called the most virtuous." [33] The
morally healthy person follows his social sentiments and is not
selfish in his moral conduct.

Thus Voltaire concludes his *Treatise* on an optimistic note
about human nature consistent with his earlier remarks on
Pascal's *Pensées*. The work remains a lasting proof that, when he
wanted to, Voltaire could be as careful and logical a thinker as
any scholastic philosopher might desire. His purpose, however,
was far from scholastic. He was forging weapons which he would
later use in an all-out war against scholasticism.

IV   *An Arsenal of Subversive Ideas:*
Philosophical Dictionary *(1764)*

The quintessence of Voltairianism is found in his one volume
"answer to the *Encyclopedia*," entitled *Philosophical Dictionary*.
This work, begun by Voltaire in the 1750s while he was living
at the court of Frederick the Great, was published in 1764, and
was periodically revised, amplified, and republished during the
later years of Voltaire's life. It consisted of a series of articles,
alphabetically arranged, on a wide variety of religious and philosophical subjects ranging from "Abraham" to "Virtue." There is
something in it to interest, and to offend, practically everybody.
For the student of Voltaire it offers a fascinating repository of
Voltaire's own learning up to the time of its publication. Here
we find Voltaire's scepticism, empiricism, and deism, which he

has drawn from native and English sources. Here is displayed the erudition that he had developed through his historical and biblical research. Here the sensitivity of the poet is admirably merged with the subtlety of the philosopher and the fervor of the religious reformer. No wonder it has been called Voltaire's most characteristic work.

As the critic Peter Gay has pointed out, the *Philosophical Dictionary* is not a dictionary but an episodic, passionate, and personal polemical tract.[34] One might add, with some justification, that it is not philosophical either, but a biased, prejudiced, propagandistic stockpile of ideas provided for the attack on Christianity, which to Voltaire was always "the Infamy" that in the name of enlightenment must be crushed. Considering its antireligious, free-thinking orientation, it is not surprising that both the work itself and its author have been vehemently attacked by Christian apologists. "It is absolutely obvious that ninety-nine per cent of Voltaire's religious writings tend to destroy, to dissolve, and to mock," writes one outraged defender of the faith.[35] Another says of Voltaire: "Sceptical, he despises not only the solutions, but the problems as well." [36] Such critics see the work more as a Devil's Dictionary rather than a Philosopher's, the product of an implacable foe of supernaturalistic religion bent upon promulgating a "final solution" to the problem of Christianity.

Peter Gay, more sympathetic to Voltaire's work, has called the *Philosophical Dictionary* "the most savage rubbish-cleaner of the age," and defends its philosophical purpose and function in that it undertakes, in line with the overall aim of the *philosophes,* the task of destroying error in order to clear the ground for the construction of newer and more substantial structures of thought and action.[37] Insofar as they are expressions of Voltaire's rigorous and sustained critical examination of human beliefs and practices, the articles in his *Dictionary* are appropriately called philosophical. Whether or not they form a coherent system of thought, the essays are philosophical in that they represent parts of an impressive attempt to relate ideals to actions, and to restore the vital continuity of means and ends. If philosophy is defined as "unified knowledge unifying life," then Voltaire's purpose was such that he could properly call his work a philosophical dictionary. Once again, it is more than just an expression of his supposed "chaos of clear ideas." It is a loosely coherent universe of examined beliefs. It is Voltaire's testimony to his agreement with Socrates that "the unexamined life is not worth living."

V   *Methodology against Madness: Voltaire's Search for Truth*

Although, unlike Descartes, Voltaire never formulated a series of "rules for the direction of the mind," such rules can easily be abstracted from a reading of his *Dictionary*. Here are some examples that suggest the methodology which underlies his work:

1. "We must repeat what Locke has so strongly urged—*Define your terms* . . . The abuse of words is an inexhaustible subject. In history, in morality, in jurisprudence, in medicine, but especially in theology, beware of ambiguity." [38]
2. "We ought often to be very uncertain of what we are certain of; and we may fail in good sense when deciding according to what is called *common* sense." [39]
3. "There are two ways of being deceived; by false judgment and self-blindness—that of erring like a man of genius, and that of deciding like a fool." "Indolent philosophy is far preferable to turbulent divinity and metaphysical delusion." [40]
4. "Disgust with our own existence, weariness of ourselves, is a malady which is likewise a cause of suicide. The remedy is a little exercise, music, hunting, the play, or an agreeable woman. The man who, in a fit of melancholy, kills himself today, would have wished to live had he waited a week." [41]

These are some of the maxims that Voltaire thinks will guide the wise person in his search for enlightenment. Be clear and unambiguous. Be sceptical. Watch out for all forms of deception. And don't take yourself or life too seriously. Learn how to divert as well as to know yourself.

Permeating his whole approach to the various "articles" in his sceptical "faith" is an irony that can, at times be as subtle as Socrates' and as devastating as Swift's. He may carefully state the intricacies of some theological dispute, not to clarify it but to reveal its absurdity. He probes into metaphysical concepts, such as the soul, not to defend them but to show their self-contradictoriness and irrelevance. Before long the reader is in on the joke, and reads on with malicious glee. Theological discourse, he surmises, does not express what is obscure by nature but is merely obscure expression. Speculative metaphysics is madness. Biblical criticism is useful only as biblical demolition. Orthodox religious beliefs and practices need to be "defined," not because they are of any value but only because they mask ignorance which must be exposed and fanaticism which must be crushed. From this point of view, Voltaire's so-called dictionary is a subversive, malicious, and witty book. It was very much inspired by the author's motto: "Laugh, and you shall crush them."

This does not mean, however, that the articles in the *Dictionary* compose a kind of philosophical jokebook. It would be more accurate to think of them as a series of indictments aimed at establishing the guilt of that "infamous thing," fanaticism.

VI   *Philosophy as the Clarification of Belief*

While in its speculative role philosophy may lead its practitioners into nonsense, in its analytical role it can lead to clarity and well-warranted beliefs. Here Voltaire is following the well-blazed trail of Bacon, Locke, and Hume. Like these empiricists and like the linguistic and analytic philosophers of today, he is more concerned with analysis than with speculation. And, as the first aphorism above suggests, this means to be aware of how words are used and abused. Many passages strike a familiar twentieth-century note as he warns thinkers to be on their guard against equivocation in the use of terms, especially in philosophy, theology, and in public affairs. "For want of defining terms, and especially for want of a clear understanding, almost all laws, that should be as plain as arithmetic and geometry, are as obscure as logogriphs." [42]

Voltaire's stress on analytic philosophy also comes through strongly in his concern, not just with critical examination of beliefs but also with the question "What is it that we call believing?" He wants to set forth criteria by which we can judge beliefs to be credible and reliable, or, in present-day terminology, to formulate criteria for determining the meaningfulness or meaninglessness, the truth or falsity of propositions. In answering such questions, Voltaire comes close to the position of the eighteenth-century philosopher David Hume and of the contemporary philosopher A. J. Ayer—that the only meaningful propositions

are those of which the truth and falsity can be determined by
the analysis of terms (i.e., analytic propositions, which are true
or false *a priori,* independently of sense experience) and those
propositions the truth or falsity of which can be determined by
referring to sense experience. (A proposition in geometry such as
"All triangles are three-sided figures" would be an example of the
first kind of proposition, and "It will rain tomorrow morning" is
an example of the second kind.)

In addition, Voltaire, again like Hume and Ayer, recognized
the meaningfulness of propositions asserting one's immediate
feelings, such as "I feel pain now." But there is also a Cartesian
note struck when Voltaire writes:

I exist, I think, I feel grief—is all that as certain as a geometrical
truth? Yes, sceptical as I am, I avow it. Why? It is that these truths
are proved by the same principle that it is impossible for a thing to
exist and not exist at the same time. I cannot at the same time feel
and not feel. A triangle cannot at the same time contain a hundred
and eighty degrees, which are the sum of two right angles, and not
contain them.[43]

Following this logic, Voltaire holds that the physical certainty
of one's existence and mathematical certainty have the same
value, even though they constitute different kinds of certainty.

Voltaire next turns to examine the second kind of proposition,
the truth or falsity of which depends upon sense verification. This
kind of proposition can never be proven to be absolutely true or
false, but only probably true or false. From all available evidence
I may believe with a high degree of certainty that the city of
Peking exists, for example, but I would never be willing to bet
my life on it with the same degree of certainty with which I
would assert that the three angles of a triangle are equal to two
right angles.[44] Belief in God would fall under this category of
belief. Voltaire never argues that one can prove rationally and
with absolute finality that a Deity exists; he argues only that,
from the evidence of design around us (i.e., the watch analogy),
we can infer the probable existence of a God (i.e., the watch-
maker). Here he differs radically from Hume and Ayer, who
would reject the view that belief in God is an empirically verifiable hypothesis.

Belief in God, then, is a belief that can be empirically

grounded; it is not, for Voltaire, simply a matter of religious faith. For faith is, in his view, more than believing what is evident. Faith is believing what is contrary to evidence; it "consists in believing not what seems true, but what seems false to our understanding." [45] (He would have appreciated Huck Finn's assertion that "Faith is believing what you know ain't so.") Faith is "the annihilation of reason, a silence of adoration at the contemplation of things absolutely incomprehensible." It is "nothing but submissive or deferential incredulity." [46] And since for him "incredulity is the basis of all knowledge" he rejects outright the validity of the truth-claims of religious faith and of dogmatic or theological metaphysics. As he had already made clear in his remarks on Pascal in his *Philosophical Letters,* he will accept only a rationally and empirically based religious belief. Here he reaffirms his conviction that to believe in God is to believe what is evident, and "it is perfectly evident" to his mind "that there exists a necessary, eternal, supreme, and intelligent being." [47]

His view of the soul in his *Dictionary* is basically the same as the one he had already formulated in his earlier *Philosophical Letters* and *Treatise on Metaphysics.* We know that we think, feel, perceive, imagine, and we have a concept of our body and of other bodies. Granted. But how can we represent to ourselves, by forming an image of an "immaterial substance," a "soul" in which the metaphysicians ask us to believe? He can neither imagine nor conceive of it. Further, he cannot conceive of how souls can be created or annihilated. For how can he or anyone know what goes beyond the knowable, that is, the empirically verifiable? To speak of the "nature of the soul" or of its "immortality," as some dogmatists do, is to speak of a fiction rather than a reality. Voltaire, at least on this topic, remains content in his scepticism. "I acknowledge, then, my ignorance; I acknowledge that four thousand volumes of metaphysics will not teach us what our soul is." [48]

VII *Voltaire's Scientific Determinism*

Freedom of the will was a meaningful concept to Voltaire when he wrote his *Treatise on Metaphysics,* but he had changed his mind by the time he wrote his *Philosophical Dictionary.* He realized that such a concept was incompatible with what he now considered to be a rational and empirically verifiable concept of reality. In his view of the universe he had become a more consistent scientific determinist; that is, he believed that every event in the universe has a determining cause, a "sufficient reason." It is absurd to speak of an uncaused event, or to speak of free will in the sense of a will that operates independently of a motive. "In this immense machine," he writes, "all is wheel, pulley, cord, or spring." [49] He goes on to clarify his position. While he accepts the interconnectedness of things, a chain of events, a system of related causes and effects, he is not saying that present events are the offspring of *all* past events. If someone sneezes in China the whole world does not catch a cold. "The events of this world form a genealogical tree"; that is, they are not the offspring of *all* past events but only of direct lines of cause and effect relationships; they have nothing to do "with a thousand small collateral lines." [50] As he puts it more fully:

Every effect evidently has its cause, ascending from cause to cause, into the abyss of eternity; but every cause has not its effect, going down to the end of ages. I grant that all events are produced one by another; if the past was pregnant with the present, the present is pregnant with the future; everything is begotten, but everything does not beget. It is a genealogical tree; every house, we know, ascends to Adam, but many of the family have died without issue. [51]

From this perspective, Voltaire thinks it is absurd to say that what occurred might not have occurred. The causes having been what they were, the effects necessarily followed. For the effects to have been different, the causes would have had to be different. "A peasant thinks that it hailed upon his field by chance; but the philosopher knows that there was no chance, and that it was absolutely impossible, according to the constitution of the world, for it not to have hailed at that very time and place." [52] Even someone who argues for such a deterministic position is "destined" to do so, just as those who oppose it also could not do otherwise. Voltaire may believe the indeterminist position to be absurd, but he claims that "many men are destined to be bad reasoners, others not to reason at all, and others to persecute those who reason well or ill." [53] Will not such a position lead to an apathetic fatalism? Why would a person bother to do anything at all, or praise or blame himself or others if he believed that he cannot do otherwise and that all of his actions, as well as those of others, are necessarily determined or "destined"? To such questions Voltaire offers no satisfactory answers.

He does not think that acceptance of determinism will cause us to lose our prejudices and passions which motivate us to act as "it is our destiny to be subjected to prejudices and passions." [54] He never seems to doubt seriously that we have the freedom to choose A rather than B; what he doubts is that we can choose one alternative rather than the other *for no reason at all.* "Will without cause is a chimera unworthy to be combatted." [55] Freedom or liberty, he never tires of repeating here and elsewhere, simply means the power of acting or the power of doing what we *will,* nothing more, nothing less. But although the concept of free will is absolutely nonsensical in his view, he does not believe that rewards and punishments for actions are undeserved or useless. A thief's nature may be such, for example, that seeing an accomplice executed may frighten him so badly, he will no longer thieve. "The punishment of his companion will become useful to him, and moreover prove to society that his will is not free." [56] Although Voltaire never seems quite satisfied with his "solution" to the extremely difficult problem of the compatibility of determinism with a certain freedom of choice, and comes back to it again and again both in his philosophical writings and in his *contes* (e.g., *Zadig*), he concludes his discussion of it in his *Dictionary* on a positive note. Sanctions can determine motives, but motives themselves cannot be undetermined.

VIII *Affirmative Deism*

Although Voltaire has sometimes been accused of being an atheist or an agnostic, it is clear from his *Dictionary* that the focal point of his entire philosophy is his belief in God. This God may be more like Aristotle's Unmoved Mover or Spinoza's Eternal Geometrician than the Jewish Jehovah, Mohammed's Allah, or the Christian's God the Father, but it is nonetheless God. Here, as in his earlier *Treatise on Metaphysics* and in his later *conte The Story of Johnny,* he devotes considerable attention to the refutation of atheism. As the arguments he gives are basically restatements of his arguments against God's existence given in his *Treatise,* they do not need to be recapitulated. They are variations on the same theme: motion cannot come from stasis; intelligence from nonintelligence; design from designlessness;

something from nothing. God's existence, though not His nature, can be inferred from the very constitution of the universe. To questions about the ultimate motives, power, and knowledge of God, Voltaire is willing to say: "I do not know," or "All I know is that we must adore Him and be just." [57]

Those who claim that the existence of evil contradicts the nature of God are presuming to know that nature. While Voltaire does not deny the existence of evil, he does deny that anyone can know the ultimate nature of God. Instead of worrying about such mysteries as why evil exists, he advises us to "console ourselves by the enjoyment of physical and moral good, and adore the Eternal Being, who has ordained the one and permitted the other." [58] The famous Voltairian dictum, "if God did not exist it would be necessary to invent Him," can be interpreted to mean that belief in God is necessary to provide a final sanction to law and morality as well as to console mortals for the sorrows of existence. Fortunately, in Voltaire's view, God is no invention of man but a divine reality, a higher intelligence, and a cosmic purpose above and beyond all things. He does not say "Believe in order to be safe and serene." His advice to the sincere religious searcher is quite different:

In the state of doubt in which we both are, I do not say to you, with Pascal, "choose the safest." There is no safety in uncertainty. We are here not to talk, but to examine; we must judge, and our judgment is not determined by our will. I do not propose to you to believe extravagant things, in order to escape embarrassment. I do not say to you, "Go to Mecca, and instruct yourself by kissing the black stone, take hold of a cow's tail, muffle yourself in a scapulary, or be imbecile and fanatical to acquire the flavor of the Being of beings." I say to you: "Continue to cultivate virtue, to be beneficent, to regard all superstition with horror, or with pity; but adore, with me, the design which is manifested in all nature, and consequently the Author of that design—the primordial and final cause of all; hope with me that our monad, which reasons on the great eternal being, may be happy, through that same great Being." [59]

Viewed from this perspective, Voltaire's *Philosophical Dictionary* is certainly not a godless or an antireligious book; it is, to the contrary, centered on the concept of God, and its deepest intention is profoundly religious. Its articles would be used as weapons to demolish religious dogma, but in the cause of promoting a higher religion. This higher religion would be notable for its simplicity, its stress on morality rather than dogma, and its lack of threats and violence to promote itself. It would teach only "the adoration of one God, justice, tolerance, and humanity." [60]

IX   *A Doubter's Credo:* The Ignorant Philosopher *(1766)*

"I am not ashamed to confess that I am ignorant of what I do not know." This statement of Cicero could well stand as a summary of Voltaire's last major attempt to state his philosophy. *The Ignorant Philosopher* is a loosely structured presentation of the aged thinker's views on a broad spectrum of problems. It begins with doubt and ends with some degree of certainty in a paean to "the Dawn of Reason." The territory it covers is basically that of his early *Treatise on Metaphysics* and its conclusions, with few exceptions, are the same. Here, as in his previous philosophical works, scepticism is the method, enlightenment the goal, and deism the pivotal doctrine. Salvation through reason is again extolled. A universal morality founded upon justice and benevolence is once more defended. But whereas his earliest treatise had been austere in its intellectual rigor and virtually devoid of all human emotion, his last is thoroughly imbued with the old *philosophe's* passion for truth, hatred for intolerance, and love of mankind.

This final profession of ignorance certainly does not preclude his confidence in a divine being. "I sink again into ignorance, which is the appendage of our nature," he intones, "and I adore that God by whom I think, without knowing how I think." [61] Further, the ignorance that he propounds is basically a sense of awareness of the limitations of finite, mortal knowledge, which should strengthen the attitudes of humility, tolerance, and desire for further inquiry. He rejects vehemently the kind of unaware ignorance that underlies dogmatism, pride, and intolerance, and supports fanaticism.

As he looks at his present age from the vantage point of most seasoned wisdom (i.e., ignorance), Voltaire finds that even with the dawn of reason "the monster, fanaticism, still exists, and whoever seeks after truth will run the risk of being persecuted."

"Must we, therefore," the ignorant philosopher concludes by asking, "remain idle in darkness, or must we light a flame, at which envy and calumny will rekindle their torches?" [62] And we know what answer the "eye of eighteenth-century illumination" gave: whatever the risk, live in the light of truth.

CHAPTER 5

Philosophy Fictionalized:
Voltaire's Contes philosophiques

A LMOST by chance Voltaire found in the philosophical tale an ideal vehicle for expressing his genius for fantasy, satire, and popularization of ideas. It was as though the imaginative author had suddenly sprung up from the Procrustean bed of neo-classicism, sprouted wings and soared across the heavens, delighting himself and the world with his aerial acrobatics. All the world loved a story, and no one could resist a story such as Voltaire could tell. From his long experience as a dramatist he knew all the tricks of the trade of plot-planning; he was a skillful wordsmith; he knew how to arouse strong emotional reactions when he wanted to; and he had a wit unmatched by any of his contemporaries. Of course, characterization was not his strong point, but who cared, so long as he could keep his puppets dancing on his strings, performing actions which were fascinating and diverting. Also, in letting his fantasy luxuriate, he realized that the tale would be the thing by which he'd catch the conscience of the public, if not of the king.

Long before Voltaire writers had written tales, and tales with a moral, but his tales were unique in that they were *philosophical*.[1] They assumed a sceptical and quizzical attitude toward humanity; they aroused the sense of wonderment over the spectacle of human life; they dealt with questions that usually were included within the domain of the sage—freedom and fate, truth and falsehood, reality and illusion, good and evil, and so on. They were so presented—and completed—that they would leave the amused reader in a reflective and questioning mood. They contributed at once to his entertainment, instruction, and enlightenment. They were intended to carry him closer to the Socratic realization that the unexamined life is not worth living.

119

Always on the lookout for a new way to further his ideas and undermine those of his enemies, the great crusher of infamous fanaticism packed into his innocent-seeming *contes* heavier and heavier ideational content. To some readers this spoiled what could have been good tales. To others the ideas he presented appeared subversive, but to Voltaire and his admirers they seemed salutary. If his characters or narrators often poked fun at authority, questioned orthodox beliefs, had experiences that were shocking, performed acts that were horrifying, he could always plead innocence himself. After all, it was they and not he who was responsible.

And so he proceeded to write stories that poked fun at human aspiration and presumption *(Memnon, Micromégas)*, that ridiculed intolerance *(Scarmentado)*, that reminded us of our vanity *(Jeannot and Colin)*, our cruelty *(An Indian Adventure, The Ingénu)*, self-deception *(The One-Eyed Porter, Candide)*, and our ignorance *(Zadig, Lord Chesterfield's Ears)*. They were written in the clear and lively style that everyone had come to expect of Voltaire. They sparkled with humor and vibrated with life. Sometimes their author got so carried away by his determination to propagandize that the magic of fantasy was dispelled. But when he successfully fused idea and tale, character and value, form and content, the result was a true work of art.

A half dozen of the most important of these *contes,* in which Voltaire fictionalized his philosophy, will be discussed in this chapter. They represent the part of his work that is most alive, most enjoyed, and most treasured today. Ironically enough, these works, upon which his reputation as an author now rests, would have been considered of secondary importance by Voltaire. Yet here, we can be sure, we have the epitome of his genius. The ease with which they were apparently written, their lightness of touch, their exuberance of spirit should not deceive the reader into thinking them examples of "easy beauty." One of Voltaire's earliest biographers, Condorcet, recognized the artistic genius which went into the making of the philosophical *conte.* As he pointed out,

This *genre* has the misfortune of appearing easy; but it requires a rare talent, that of knowing how to express by a play of wit and of imagination, or even by the very events of a story, the results of a profound philosophy without ceasing to be natural and how to be pungent without ceasing to be true. One has to be a philosopher yet not seem to be one.[2]

I   *Free or Fated?* Zadig *(1747)*

In *Zadig or Destiny*, which appeared in 1747, Voltaire, in an oriental setting, raises the problem of human freedom and determinism. Masquerading as a fable out of *A Thousand and One Nights*, with touches of fantasy such as a talking parrot and an angel disguised as a hermit, the story—as the author tells us in a prefatory epistle—was written for the purpose of conveying a philosophical message.

It introduces a hero who, in his search for happiness, runs into endless obstacles, seemingly put in his way by a hostile fate. Zadig, whose name means "just" in Arabic and who consistently represents mankind at its best, wishes only to do good, but is victimized at every turn by human greed, envy, and prejudice. Intermittently, however, his exceptional qualities are recognized by influential personages, who take him into their confidence and elevate him to high positions. Thus we see a confused protagonist continually tossed back and forth by the winds of fortune between the heights and depths of human existence, unable to make sense of a world where evil almost invariably wins out over good. Eventually he learns that the events he attributed to mere chance are in reality part of an overall design invisible to man, but arranged to his ultimate benefit by an all-powerful Providence.

Voltaire might have entitled his story: *Zadig or All's Well That Ends Well*, for the hero ends up with the happiness he so richly deserves, King of Babylon and married to the queen he loves, while the wicked are punished according to their just deserts. Hovering over Zadig is an inscrutable Providence which always knows best, whose strange and often offensive ways should not be questioned but accepted as necessary and right. The implication is that from a higher philosophical perspective all is indeed for the best in the best of all possible worlds. In the story, Voltaire does not condone the existence of evil, but accepts it as an inevitable ingredient in the world as it is. For a world without evil, as the angel later explains to Zadig, would be a different world in which events would be linked according to a different divine plan.

Zadig's enlightenment comes after a long series of trials. We meet him first in Babylon, a well-educated, well-balanced, sensitive young man who has everything except experience, as is evidenced by his naive belief that he can be happy *because* he possesses wealth, health, good looks, an innate sense of justice, and a sincere heart.[3] He will soon learn that his superior qualities are no guarantee or, in Leibnizian language, a "sufficient reason" for felicity.

He begins by seeking happiness in love (a passion that rarely fares well in Voltaire's hands). Almost immediately he is disillusioned: his fiancée abandons him for a rival and his wife betrays him at the first opportunity. He then turns to the study of nature as a more reliable source of contentment, for "Nothing is happier . . . than a philosopher who reads in the great book that God has put under our eyes. The truths he discovers are his; he nourishes and elevates his soul; he lives in peace. . . ."[4]

Again he has reckoned without the world. While tales of his uncommon intelligence spread to the royal court, his knowledge also arouses the suspicion of the King's judges, who condemn him for crimes he has never committed.

Philosophy and friendship, the next roads he explores, bring him only the envy of neighbors; unable to match either his wisdom or his humanity, they succeed in having him arrested for *lèse majesté*. Escaping execution only by a miracle, our bewildered hero next finds himself Prime Minister, a favorite of the King and Queen, and honored by all who know him.

Under the illusion that he has reached his goal, an unsuspecting Zadig changes his former complaint about the elusiveness of happiness to the conviction that it is not so hard to find, after all. Zadig's very happiness, however, becomes the cause of his downfall. The Prime Minister and the Queen conceive a passion for each other; that passion produces the jealousy of the King; the jealousy, in turn, obliges Zadig to flee from Babylon for his life. Man may propose but Providence disposes. What an imperfect human mistakes for chance occurrences are, in fact, so many links in the unbroken chain that charts his destiny. There is a secret logic in the chain of events that lead to an inevitable outcome.

Unaware of the necessity of his misfortunes, Zadig is powerless to do anything but lament them. From now on he is a wanderer, alternately praised and reviled, now a slave, then an honored counselor, protected by the discerning who recognize his value, denounced and persecuted by those who, dominated by their vices, envy and fear him.

At all times Zadig remains true to himself and to his name, a champion of justice, spreading enlightenment wherever he goes by speaking the "language of reason." Every good deed he performs produces two contrary results: gratitude and envy. He endears himself forever to young Arabian widows for saving them from being burnt on their husbands' funeral pyres, but arouses the wrath of the priests who habitually enriched themselves by confiscating their victims' jewels. He incurs the ire of the fraudulent medical profession by curing a sick man through natural means; and he implicitly earns the undying hatred of every priesthood, Oriental and Western, by exposing superstition at a trade fair, where he convinces adherents of different religions that, whatever their ritual, they all adore the same God.

This dichotomy is apparent throughout the story. It is manifest in the juxtaposition of a just man and an unjust world. It further shows itself in the contrast between what appears to be a chaotic world and a well-ordered universe. For example, Zadig is continually struck by the contrast between the reality of his own sorrows on earth and their insignificance in the context of the infinite. Contemplating the constellations in a vast sky, he sees "men for what they are . . .: insects devouring each other on a little atom of mud." [5] Yet when he thinks back on his own situation, "the universe disappeared from his sight," and it ceases to be a consolation.[6] Finally this double aspect is present in Zadig himself. Rising above himself when dealing with others and a constant inspiration to those who seek his help, he is profoundly unhappy in his private life. Grief-stricken over the loss of his queen, he cannot reconcile himself to a world order that seems to ignore virtue and recompense vice. More and more he is struck by the discrepancy between a man's good actions and their often bad consequences. His reflections make him miserable, a rebel without a cause.

While his revolt is continuous, its target shifts imperceptibly. What begins as his disenchantment with the behavior of his fellowmen changes to a protest against a capricious fate, until he finally dares to point an accusing finger at Providence itself. His voice becomes that of an anguished humanity taking issue with a God whom he, the just man, considers unjust. This alternation

shows itself clearly in his reflections on his experiences. Thus,
after hearing from a prosperous robber that Babylon has been
sacked, the king killed, and the queen captured, he ponders the
meaning of a universe in which thieves are made happy and
"the loveliest creature nature ever made may have perished in
the most horrible way, or else lives in a state worse than death." [7]
A little later he is "deploring his destiny," and soon after he
remarks, on the subject of evil-doers, that "usually it is these
people who are destiny's favorites." [8] He continues from there
finally to "accuse" his fate, a man in revolt.

By a seeming reversal of that same fate, however, he finds his
long-lost queen when he least expects it, and in due course joins
her in Babylon. But the chosen are tested to the bitter end, and
when happiness is practically within reach the hero is once more
separated from the woman he loves by the trickery of others.
This final blow is too cruel for him to bear, and for the first time
he rebels against divinity itself; we see him wandering along the
banks of the Euphrates, "filled with despair and secretly accusing
Providence, which was forever persecuting him." [9]

It is at this crucial moment that he meets the hermit, an old
man "whose white and venerable beard reached to his waist,"
absorbed in reading a book. Impressed by the stranger's kind
and noble looks (a reflection, although Zadig does not know it,
of his divine benevolence), he engages him in conversation and
learns that the stranger is perusing the book of destinies. He
accepts an invitation to have a look at it, but to his surprise
cannot decipher a single letter, despite his competence in foreign
languages. As in *Micromégas,* the book of divine wisdom must
remain a mystery to humans.

The hermit persuades Zadig to accompany him and to stick
by him no matter what happens. It is here that the hero, still
unsuspecting, is initiated into the secret workings of Providence.
He watches his saintly friend stealing from a generous host,
rewarding a miser, setting fire to the house of a virtuous philosopher, and drowning the fourteen-year-old nephew of a chari-
table widow. Unable to comprehend what he considers senseless
and indeed criminal acts, a scandalized Zadig explodes in bitter
reproaches. In return the hermit reveals the reasons behind his
inexplicable deeds: the first man had to be punished for his
vanity, the second made aware of his avarice; the philosopher
was due to find a treasure under the ruins of his house; and had

the young boy been allowed to live, he would have murdered his aunt within a year and Zadig within two.

To understand, however, is not to approve. Again Zadig speaks with the voice of an enlightened humanity, unable to stand idly by while seeming injustices take place before his eyes. "Who told you so, barbarian?," he cries in indignation. "And even if you had read this in your book of destinies, are you allowed to drown a child who has not done you any harm?" [10] He thus expresses man's eternal quarrel with the unacceptable ways of a higher order which he is destined never to penetrate; Zadig speaks as a mortal whose imperfect sight can only perceive part of the whole, but whose very anger is a credit to humanity.

The discussion stops abruptly, however, when the hermit assumes his true identity by changing into an angel; for man does not dare converse with heaven. Zadig is told to submit and to adore—a precept repeated over and over in Voltaire—and he can only obey. Nevertheless, nagging questions persist, and even as the hero prepares to prostrate himself, he pronounces the characteristic Voltairian "But. . . ." The significance of this lies in the uttering, with its implied rejection of things as they are and its desire for a better order.

The answer to this recurring protest, however, is never given. Voltaire thus leaves open the question of free will in a universe in which, as the angel has explained, ". . . there is no chance: everything is a test, or a punishment, or a reward or foresight." [11]

If everything is prearranged, what happens to human freedom? The question of free will always preoccupied Voltaire; we have seen how, as the years passed he became more and more of a determinist. He grants man very little freedom of choice in *The Ignorant Philosopher*, but in *Zadig* man's freedom still seems to lie in his ability to choose between good and evil. It is because he was virtuous that Zadig is rewarded and made happy in the end. It is an optimistic conclusion, indicating Voltaire's belief in the ultimate triumph of justice—a quality he considered innate and universal.

"The wicked," the angel informs Zadig, "are always unhappy; they serve to test a small number of just men scattered over the earth, and there is no evil from which some good does not result." [12]

Twelve years later, in *Candide*, the wicked will not be unhappy, and the only good man in the story will be drowned by a scoundrel. And in 1767 Voltaire ends his *Ingénu* by declaring that many honest people in this world derive no good of any kind from their misfortunes.

But then, in the years between *Zadig* and these later stories Madame du Châtelet had died, Voltaire had returned in disgrace from Berlin to a France which declared him unwelcome, and the Lisbon earthquake had shaken, along with the walls of that city, his belief in a benevolent Providence to its very foundations.

We can be reasonably sure that Zadig's happiness was but a brief glow of light in a world increasingly darkened by evil, allowed to flourish undisturbed by an unconcerned Providence. That light will never be entirely extinguished, but it will change from the bright chandeliers in Zadig's palace to the flickering lantern in Candide's garden.

II *Presumptuous Humans:* Micromégas (1752)

A light-hearted story of interplanetary travel, *Micromégas* was written in 1752 during Voltaire's stay at the Prussian court, although it was probably conceived in the early Cirey years when the poet was engrossed in study. The little tale reflects his preoccupations, for it is permeated from one end to the other by science and philosophy. The main inspirations are Alexander Pope, whose recent *Essay on Man* stressed the divine harmony in nature, and Newton's discoveries about the laws governing outer space. Also in evidence are Locke and Voltaire's old friend Swift, echoes of whose *Gulliver's Travels* are easily recognizable. Rabelais cannot have been far from the author's mind when he created his giant protagonist, and the fantastic voyage the giant undertakes resembles similar exploits imagined by Cyrano de Bergerac. Despite this variety of sources the end product is pure Voltaire, in spirit as in style.

Micromégas is a philosophical inquiry into man's place in the universe. How important is man? Is he the crown of creation, as he is wont to believe, or an insignificant speck in the void that engulfs him? Where does he belong in the scheme of things? What account can mankind give of itself? In order to arrive at an impartial answer to these questions Voltaire invents a visitor from another planet, Micromégas, who subjects the tiny race that inhabits the earth to thorough examination. The final conclusion is suggested by the hero's name, which means "Small-Big," indicating that all size is relative. *Micromégas* might be called a study in perspective, with creatures appearing big or small according to the dimensions of the observer. Man may be almost invisible to mammoth beings from outer space, but he grows into a colossus compared to the tiny animals crawling around in a drop of water, which he can perceive only with the help of a microscope.

Size, however, is not Voltaire's only or even main considera-tion. Given that each creature is proportioned to his environment —a main tenet of the story—the need is to recognize that fact. Voltaire, like Pascal before him, places man between two infinites—the infinitely big and the infinitely small. But Voltaire's man, unlike his Pascalian predecessor, is not asked to feel an-guish at this precarious, midway position. Instead, he is asked to realize the ridiculousness of the human inclination to believe that everything around him has been created for his benefit. By holding such an absurd view, Voltaire implies, man assigns him-self an importance he does not and can not have in the scheme of things. As soon as man begins to see himself as godlike, he becomes ridiculous. In his own easy, mocking way Voltaire here follows Pascal and pulls man down when he wants to play the angel. He does this by creating a Sirian giant by whom the puny humans are carefully scrutinized.

Micromégas is eminently qualified for his role as an unbiased judge. Not belonging to the human race, he is free of its preju-dices, yet he is sufficiently akin to it so as to make communication possible. An inhabitant of one of the planets turning around Sirius, he measures one hundred and twenty thousand feet in height—dimensions unimaginable to a man but in perfect har-mony with those of his planet. Apart from their size, Sirians are not very different from humans, and striking similarities exist between the protagonist and the author. Like Voltaire, for in-stance, Micromégas is in trouble with his country's censors; he has been banned from the Sirian court for eight hundred years for having written a book supposedly containing heretical state-ments, and therefore condemned by some of his fellow Sirians

who have never read it. It is to educate himself during his exile
that the young man—barely four hundred and fifty years old—
decides on his "philosophical journey" through space.

Again like Voltaire, he is well acquainted with Newton's law
of attraction and repulsion; by using sun rays and comets as his
means of transportation, he moves easily from planet to planet
"as a bird flutters from branch to branch." [13] Having the same
philosophical bent of mind as his creator, he is not surprised at
encountering creatures different from himself, to whom he is
willing to grant equal intelligence even if they are much inferior
in size. Thus he realizes that a scholar he meets on Saturn "is
not necessarily ridiculous just because he is only six thousand
feet tall." [14] The lesson here is to accept nature's "astonishing
variety."

Secretary of the local Academy of Science, the Saturnian becomes the Sirian's travel companion and fellow observer of the
human race. Because of his diminutiveness he is referred to
throughout the story as "the dwarf from Saturn"—a condescen-
sion that is not accidental, for the Saturnian is modeled on the
French writer and critic Fontenelle, Perpetual Secretary of the
Academy of Science in Paris, and author of a popularized as-
tronomy book for the use of well-born ladies, *Conversations on
the Plurality of Worlds*. Voltaire ridicules his colleague's flowery
language, meant to "please" the so-called weaker sex rather than
"instruct" the serious student. With some malice he describes
his "dwarf" as "a man of great wit who, to tell the truth, had
not invented anything but who could give good accounts of the
inventions of others, and was fairly apt at making little verses
and big calculations." [15]

Before their arrival on our planet, the two space travelers
have a revealing discussion concerning their relative condition.
The reader learns that Saturnians have only seventy-two senses
as compared to close to one thousand for the Sirians. They live
no more than fifteen thousand years, whereas the Sirians' life-
span is seven hundred times as long. All things being relative,
their complaints are the same: both are aware of their physical
and mental limitations, and both deplore the fact that their
existence passes in a flash and that death arrives almost at the
moment of birth. They agree, however, that the Creator has
proportioned everything just right and that everywhere in nature
a divine plan is manifest.

Thus mentally prepared, the two finally arrive on the planet Earth, which they circle on foot in thirty-six hours without discovering any sign of habitation. The dwarf, always a little hasty in his conclusions, decides that no life exists on the tiny globe since no creature in his right mind would want to inhabit such an irregular surface even if he could. The Sirian's reply serves as an introduction to the human race: he remarks that earthlings might well be creatures out of their right mind.

The stage is now set for the encounter between man and his extraterrestrial visitors. The great trial of humanity is about to take place. On its performance will depend the judgment not only of the Sirian philosopher, but of every enlightened member of its own species.

Voltaire places his story in July, 1737, just when the French scientist Maupertuis, still a friend of his at that time, was returning from his famous expedition to Lapland where he had gone to measure the earth's curvature at the North Pole. With him were traveling some of France's most distinguished scientists. Since it is their ship that Micromégas manages to lift, with great care, out of the Baltic Sea, he has the good luck of being able to converse with humanity's most illustrious representatives.

Filled with compassion for a race of such minuscule proportions, the Sirian giant opens the dialogue by offering his protection to the "invisible insects it has pleased the Maker to create in the abyss of the infinitely small." [16] He then proceeds to question them on two counts: their knowledge and their way of life.

It soon becomes evident that humans are endowed with great intelligence. They master physics and mathematics, and are able to measure and calculate the world outside them with amazing accuracy. They know the distance between their planet and the moon, and can weigh water and air. Consequently the Sirian conceives a great esteem for them. But his favorable opinion changes when he discovers that human knowledge is limited to the exact sciences, where conclusions are verifiable. For as soon as the tiny beings are questioned about themselves, confusion spreads. They are quick to answer the giant's questions about the soul and the origin of thought, but do not agree among themselves; every one has a different opinion. More distressing than their ignorance, however, is their presumption, for each of them insists that he alone is right. Only a disciple of Locke is willing to admit that there is much man will never know, but his modesty is an exception.

Man's reason, then, is clearly imperfect. What of his existence? How does he fill the fleeting moment on earth that has been allotted to him? Micromégas tells the human atoms: ". . . no doubt you taste very pure joys on your globe, for having so little matter and appearing all mind, you must spend your lives loving and thinking, which is the true life of the spirit." [17]

What follows is Voltaire's familiar description of humanity. Here, as in his other *contes,* he presents humanity as "a bunch of madmen, villains, and wretches" who spend their time killing or being killed by each other.[18] Micromégas' former compassion changes to indignation, then back to pity for this weak, defective species. Man's fault lies not in his imperfection, however, for this is the way he has been created. His great sin lies elsewhere and is revealed by a theologian aboard ship, "an animalcule in a doctor's cap." This sage claims to know the secret of all things. Eyeing his visitors from outer space up and down as far as his feeble sight will allow, he declares solemnly that both of them, as well as their planets, their suns, their stars, and everything else were created solely for the benefit of man. At this the two giants burst into homeric laughter and leave the human race to its fate.

As a farewell present, Micromégas gives his human friends a philosophy book, written in small letters for their special use, in which the purpose of all things is explained. But when it is officially opened by the Secretary of the Academy in Paris, the latter sees only blank pages. No more than his fellow men, does he possess the capacity to read the book of destiny. Men, in other words, cannot and should not attempt to go beyond their inborn limits.

Voltaire conveys this message with much good humor, and refrains from condemning the human race for its presumption. At most he participates in the final mocking laughter of the space-visitors. All he asks of mankind is to stop seeing itself as the center of creation, and abandon a notion discredited long ago by Galileo. Once man comes to his astronomical senses, he will be able to say with the angel Babouc in *The World As It Goes* that if all is not well with his world, all is at least tolerable.

III *Lashing Optimism:* Candide

If *Candide* is generally conceded to be Voltaire's masterpiece, it is not because it contains new ideas, nor because its style differs in any important way from that of the other *contes*. Voltaire reiterates what he has stated many times before, in the same rapid, easy-flowing style that characterizes all his prose. What makes *Candide* superior is a breadth of vision and a blending of form with content, sustained without a break through thirty chapters, that give it a solidity and an artistic unity not found to this extent in Voltaire's other fiction. Since its appearance in 1759 right up until today, *Candide or Optimism,* supposedly "translated from the German of Dr. Ralph," has not only been enormously popular but also the subject of continual critical discussion. Among the recent commentators, Jean Sareil has drawn attention to the fact that, in *Candide,* Deity is absent and Voltaire considers the world strictly from man's point of view.[19] René Pomeau has ascribed the work's originality to a "continuity of perfection"[20] while Ira Wade regards it as "the summary of all Voltaire's past" and "a blueprint for works of the remainder of his life."[21]

We can still feel the revelance of *Candide* to our human condition because, as Sareil rightly emphasized, in it Voltaire deals solely with man. Gone are *Micromégas'* giants from outer space, *Zadig's* talking birds, and angels in disguise, material evidence of a Providence hitherto assumed, if with less and less conviction, to be ultimately benevolent. Pascal's silent heavens no longer play a role, for Voltaire has given up questioning them for nonexisting answers. He now speaks as a man to his fellowmen about the human race and the world it has made for itself. If that world is none too good, the fault is chiefly man's. In essence, Voltaire echoes the words of his enemy Jean-Jacques Rousseau: "Men, all your misfortunes come from you!" Unlike Rousseau, however, he proposes no sweeping plan to change society through changing man.

In its broadest sense, the subject of *Candide* is innocent man's experience of a mad and evil world, his struggle to survive in that world, and, eventually, to come to terms with it and create his own existence within it. The same may be true, to some extent, of *Zadig* and *The Ingénu,* but there the field of vision is smaller and the solutions are tailor-made to suit the individual protagonist in every case. The superiority of *Candide* lies in its universality, in its epic proportions.

Basically, it has two things to say: the reality is bad; but the denial of that reality is even worse. If the world is wicked, let us at least not pretend that it is good, for that will not help us to cope with it. In *Candide* Voltaire shows us a world filled with catastrophes, sometimes natural but mostly man-made, and contrasts it with a philosophy that maintains, against all evidence, that all is well and could not, in fact, be better. The philosophy in this case is Leibniz's postulation that all is for the best in the best of all possible worlds, a metaphysical optimism summed up in Pope's famous aphorism, "Whatever is, is right."

Neither Voltaire's experience nor circumstances inclined him to support such a view. He was wary of philosophical systems in general because they dealt in abstractions and did not, therefore, correspond to the reality of life—the only thing that concerned him. In 1758 a philosophy of optimism was the last thing that could appeal to him: he still smarted from the treatment received at the hands of both Louis XV and Frederick; the horror of the Lisbon earthquake was indelibly imprinted on his mind; and all around him he saw Europe being ravaged by a senseless and bloody war. Seizing therefore upon the German philosopher's metaphysical speculation, which he embodied in the character of Dr. Pangloss, he held it up to the light of experience and there exposed it in all its cruel absurdity.

This satire of the human predicament is presented in the form of a love story mixed with travelogue. We follow young Candide, the hero, in his quest for Cunégonde, daughter of the German Baron of Thunder-ten-Tronckh, whom he loves, whom he loses at the end of the first chapter, and in search of whom he travels halfway around the world. Characters assisting the story's two protagonists include some of their fellow inhabitants of the Baron's castle: Cunégonde's arrogant brother who remains unnamed and whose homosexuality is hinted at, the chambermaid Paquette whose indiscriminate favors spread love and disease in equal proportion, and, most important, Dr. Pangloss, the "greatest philosopher in the province and consequently in the whole world," who teaches "metaphysico-theologo-cosmolo-nonsense." They are joined later by the South American half-breed Cacambo, faithful servant-of-all-trades; the pessimist Martin, a Manichean

who believes in the predominance of evil and is thus a counter-
poise to the optimistic Pangloss; and the one-buttocked Old
Woman, daughter of a Pope and a Princess, whom dire misfortunes have reduced to the state of a servant. All play their
assigned parts somewhat like marionettes, appearing, disappear-
ing, and reappearing at their creator's will; only Candide, the
innocent hero-victim, is present throughout. Dominating the
whole is master Pangloss; though he is physically absent from
the scene most of the time, it is his spirit that dominates the story
and gives it its meaning.

This learned doctor believes in the principle of "sufficient
reason," the basis of Leibnizian determinism, or, in plain language, that there is no effect without cause. Things, he declares,
cannot be different from what they are, and since everything
exists for a purpose, it is necessarily for the best purpose. He
"proves" it admirably. "Notice," he lectures, "that noses were
created to support glasses; therefore we wear glasses. Legs were
obviously invented to be hosed, and so we have hose . . . and
since pigs were made to be eaten, we eat pork every day of the
year." [22] (The latter example is meant as a slap at German
cuisine; Voltaire's frequent unflattering allusions to things Teu-
tonic were his revenge on Frederick.) Pangloss's conclusion
reverberates all through *Candide* as an increasingly dissonant
refrain: "Consequently, those who have declared that all is well,
have talked nonsense: they should have said that all is for the
best." [23] The doctor sticks rigidly to his thesis, unswayed by all
evidence to the contrary. Though disfigured by syphilis (for
Pangloss loves women as much as he does philosophy), hanged,
dissected, thrashed, and made a galley slave, he insists that things
could not be better "because after all . . . I am a philosopher
and it is not fitting that I should contradict myself." [24]

The innocent Candide unquestioningly accepts his master's
doctrine; he has indeed no reason to doubt its veracity so long as
he lives under the same roof with his Cunégonde. True love
seems to have no place in the best of all possible worlds, however, for no sooner has the hero received the first kiss from his
beloved, than he is bodily kicked out of his earthly paradise. On
his own in the outside world, he will now be forced to compare
the theory with the facts.

In no other work has Voltaire given vent to his feelings with
such satanic glee; Flaubert called it a "grinding of teeth." In

Candide's world there is no evil that does not flourish, no crime that is not committed, no abomination that is not routinely perpetrated. He unleashes upon his hero a long series of unmitigated disasters, interrupted only here and there by an unexpected encounter with the elusive Cunégonde, lost again almost as soon as she is found, and by a short stopover in a never-never land where perfection proves to be as unbearable as the chaos that reigns elsewhere.

The reader escapes the full impact of the horrors recounted only through a mixture of comic effects obtained by various means. Voltaire's tabulations and exaggerations, for instance, reflect a distorting mirror image of the world rather than a true picture; Pangloss's pseudo-erudition and the unfailing irrelevance of his remarks transform philosophy into gibberish and the philosopher himself into a buffoon; Candide's two-dimensional stature, finally, makes him less react to facts than register them, and so reduces him just enough to a character in a Punch and Judy show to prevent the audience from identifying with him.

The hero needs this protection against suffering as much as the sympathetic reader, for Voltaire spares Candide none of the trickery used by man to torment his neighbor. Thus we see him forcibly inducted into the Bulgarian army, starving in Holland, refused private charity by those who preach it publicly, wounded in the Lisbon earthquake (when nature adds her share to human distress), arrested by the Holy Inquisition (a favorite target of Voltaire's, at the hands of which many of his heroes are made to suffer), and beaten rhythmically for public entertainment in an *auto-da-fé*. What sustains him in his trials is the thing men live by and find it hardest to abandon: hope. Despite his experiences, Candide remains faithful to his master's credo, and keeps expecting things to be better elsewhere—almost till the very end. When reality gets the better of him and doubts begin to assail his mind, an unexpected incident may restore his faith temporarily. When, for instance, he is ready to reject a best of all possible worlds in which he sees his former master hanged by order of the Grand Inquisitor, he is made to believe in it once more with the reappearance of Cunégonde, previously reported dead; a much-violated Cunégonde, it is true, much used and abused, but as alluring as ever and faithful to the hero in her fashion.

Cunégonde becomes his reason for living, symbol of love, personification of hope, incarnation of that best of all possible worlds. It is for her that he will endure hardship, for her that he will leave the happy land of Eldorado, for union with her that he is ready to wait.

Wait he must, for romance cannot blossom in the wasteland of *Candide,* where any reunion is only a prelude to another separation. For when the couple has reached the New World— which, not surprisingly, proves as much of a disillusion as the old one they left behind—Cunégonde, the eternal Woman, exchanges an old love for a new one; more specifically she abandons Candide for the mustachioed Governor of Argentina, Don Fernando d'Ibaraa, y Figueora, y Macarenes, y Lampourdos, y Souza, whose Spanish pride is as fierce as his name is resounding, and who has an unfailing eye for female beauty. To our hero she must remain both an illusion and a reality, pursued and yearned for as long as she remains the former, but, like every reality in the story, undesirable and undesired when she finally reemerges, soured and faded. Her transformation is Voltaire's last act of destruction—an inevitable one, without which he cannot begin his ultimate work of reconstruction.

The road leading to that point is long and strewn with corpses. There is no segment of society that Voltaire, inconoclastic to the core, does not leave eviscerated in *Candide;* no sacred cow whose hollow insides he does not expose, no imposing edifice he does not reduce to a heap of rubble. Unlike its predecessor and spiritual cousin, the *Philosophical Letters, Candide* offers no alternatives for what it tears down. For the present the moral universe appears to be shattered. What substitutes can be given when faith in humanity has collapsed? Voltaire himself is speaking when Candide asks his friend Martin: "Do you think men have always massacred each other as they do today? That they have always been liars, scoundrels, traitors, ingrates, robbers, weaklings, cheats, cowards, enviers, gluttons, drunkards, misers, climbers, blood-thirsty, slanderers, libertines, fanatics, hypocrites, and fools?" [25] And it is Voltaire who has Martin ask in return: "Do you think that hawks have always eaten pigeons when they found any? . . . if hawks have always had the same nature, why should men have changed theirs?"

The question appears rhetorical, yet Voltaire shrinks before such a wholesale condemnation; Martin, after all is as frozen in his pessimism as Pangloss is in his opposite philosophy. Therefore he has Candide exclaim, "Oh, there is indeed a great difference, for man possesses free will. . . ." [26] He will go no farther, however; his characters engage in a lengthy discussion on the matter, without deciding for or against. Communication here is more important than reaching a conclusion. Ira Wade has drawn attention to the duplicity of *Candide,* in the sense that it is "in its inner substance not *wholly* optimistic, or pessimistic, or sceptical, or cynical but all of these things at the same time." [27] The final garden, flourishing on Voltaire's ruins, is the concrete image of creation and destruction existing side by side, with creation, being alive with growth, winning out. Life is ultimately stronger, more stubborn than demolition.

Joining the hero in his travels, we may note some of Voltaire's targets. The list is almost endless. Social injustice, religious oppression, medical fraud and quackery, legal corruption, class snobbery, court flattery, slavery, tyranny, prostitution, syphilis, and ubiquitous greed, hypocrisy, and stupidity—nothing escapes his lethal pen.

The Jesuits' brutal rule in Paraguay, for example, is described by Cacambo as "something admirable. Their kingdom is more than three hundred miles in diameter. Los Padres have everything, and the people nothing; it is a masterpiece of reason and justice." [28] In the South American jungle there is, again in the words of Cacambo, "nothing more fair" than the cannibalism practiced by the native savages, because "natural right teaches us to kill our neighbor, and this is the way people act everywhere on earth." [29] From a mutilated Surinam Negro we learn that mutilation is a routine punishment for any slave who tries to escape from forced labor in the sugar fields. "It is at that price," remarks the victim, "that you people eat sugar in Europe." [30] The English kill their own admirals for losing battles because ". . . in this country it is a good thing to kill an admiral from time to time to encourage the others." [31] The French can only get along with each other at supper time, when they are busy eating, "all the rest of the time is spent in senseless quarrels: Jansenists against Molinists, lawyers against churchmen, men of letters against men of letters, courtiers against courtiers, tax collectors against the people, wives against husbands, relatives against relatives; it's an eternal war." [32]

In the midst of this global desolation Voltaire creates the country of Eldorado, located in Peru, on the site of the ancient

Inca kingdom, cut off from the rest of the world by inaccessible mountains. Corruption has not been able to enter this earthly paradise. It would have no reason for existing, for there is no poverty and no inequity, hence no greed and no crime. Everyone has enough; everyone is happy. The one religion consists of thanking God for his bounty, and each person acts as his own priest. Contrary to all expectation, we seem to have arrived in the best of all possible worlds; Pangloss appears vindicated, though the good doctor is not there to see it.

A closer look reveals, however, that Eldorado is as much satire as the rest of the story; for all its reality within the narrative, it does not exist outside it. A sage aged one hundred and seventy-two years living in a "simple" house decorated with silver, gold, emeralds, and rubies, public buildings reaching to the sky, fountains of clear water, rose water, and sugar cane juice, gold lying uncoveted on the streets in the form of mud and pebbles—all these, after all, are no more realistically acceptable than the miraculous resuscitations from the dead of Pangloss and other characters elsewhere in the story. The psychological aspect of this enchanted land is equally unsuited to human nature; where every desire is gratified almost before it can be formulated, man is left with only time on his hands. It is that most unbearable of all situations, Pascal's state of complete repose. It is an absolute, like death and the sun which, as La Rochefoucauld knew, we cannot look at directly. So that, in the greatest ironic twist of all, Voltaire proves his philosopher right, then wrong after all, for even the best of all possible worlds turns out to be unfit for humans and no more than an idyllic tourist spot where man can, at best, spend a short vacation.

Human inability to be happy in the absence of challenge is also illustrated vividly, in the real world this time, by the nobleman Pococurante, whose private Eldorado is located not behind rugged mountain peaks, but among the stagnant waters of Venice. The Venetian senator, cultured but sated, consumed by ennui but unable to make his escape, has everything except desires; in the static splendor of his precious possessions life has come to a full stop. The purified air in his elegant Venetian garden is as unbreathable as it was in its South American counterpart.

The question facing humanity, then, is to find a middle way between what Martin calls the "convulsions of anxiety" and the "lethargy of boredom." This is the basic problem Candide and

his friends have to deal with once their ordeal is over, when they
have a place of their own at last. Life becomes an existential
problem.

Man cannot live by destruction alone. Once everything has
been demolished, once the earth has been cleansed of its sins
and every barrier to human freedom has been smashed, what do
we do? Candide and his friends do not know right away. They
waste time philosophizing and do nothing, while the burden of
action falls on one person, Cacambo, who cannot by himself
manage the responsibilities of all. It is the complaint of the Old
Woman that sufferings might, after all, be more easily bearable
than deadening boredom, the art of survival being, in the long
run, more essentially creative than mere existence. Her words
set Candide thinking and lead to his solution to the fundamental
problem that every man faces at all times: what to do with the
life allotted to him.

Voltaire, who had defended humanity against Pascal in 1734,
chooses life in defiance of all the odds in *Candide*. Having created
a wasteland, he is now ready for the business of reconstruction.
Negative action becomes positive action. For every action is
creation, and creation is life itself. Candide, wizened by experience, knows that the great ideals of love and happiness belong to
the world of abstract reasoning, in which Pangloss never ceases
to shine. Yet, living itself is love and happiness, if we can only
define our terms. The real Eldorado is in Candide's garden, which
is small but which yields a great deal if it is tended to properly.
Collective effort, each according to his talents, is the only way
man can hope to create a society in which he can live with a
minimum of contentment.

Voltaire's conclusion, "We must cultivate our garden," is at
one and the same time his most modest and most sweeping
statement. Work not only eliminates the three great curses of
mankind—want, boredom, and vice—it also transforms the
chronological sequence of a lifetime, in itself a mere elapsing
of time, into a creation that constantly renews itself, indeed,
must renew itself in order to remain a creation.

Certain conditions must be fulfilled. Man must love his fellow-
man and be just, for individual morality is the basis of every human society worthy of the name. He must also be vigilant, lest
weeds overgrow his garden, choke its growth, and turn it back
into a primitive jungle; above all, he must keep from useless

theorizing, for that will not teach him that most important task of all: the art of living. Resigned in the end to accepting an absurd reality—there is no viable alternative—Voltaire shows us how to make the best of a bad situation and suggests that, on a small scale at least, improvement may be possible.

This is the lesson taught by *Candide*. If it still seems relevant today, it is because mankind remains very much the same and is as far from achieving the story's modest goal as it was in Voltaire's time.

IV   *The Uses of Misfortune:* The Ingénu *(1767)*

The Ingénu (L'Ingénu), the last of Voltaire's four best-known *contes*, appeared in 1767, almost ten years after *Candide*. The heroes of these two tales have in common a basic innocence which derives from their lack of experience with the world around them—a quality which they share to some extent also with their predecessors Zadig and Micromégas. The name "L'Ingénu"—that of the protagonist as well as the story—can, like "Candide" be translated as "the artless one," referring to the straightforward, honest hero who has acquired none of the undesirable traits that have become associated with the so-called civilized man. As in his other stories, Voltaire here opposes the innate goodness of an individual to the chicanery of the collective body of individuals that constitute society.

There is, however, an added element. The present hero is not merely without guile; he is also a primitive, for he has been brought up among the Indians of the New World. We are dealing, therefore, not just with innocence versus intrigue, but with the simple man of nature caught up in the complexities of a highly developed social system.

The myth of the Noble Savage, born free of civilization and following only nature's ways, captivated many eighteenth-century writers, particularly Rousseau. Voltaire was more critical. He was willing enough to do away with the evils of civilization, but not with civilization itself. His *Ingénu* is consequently both an attack on and a defense of society and, by extension, both a glorification and a criticism of "natural" but uncultivated man. In the end society wins out, for despite the injustices he has suffered the main character opts for civilized society. Having gained the knowledge and insight Voltaire judged indispensable to being

a "modern" (i.e., eighteenth-century) man, the former Savage
feels transformed, in his own words, "from a brute into a man." [33]
He will henceforth take his place in an enlightened generation
that will spearhead the struggle for human progress. Thus *The
Ingénu* is not merely a novel of condemnation; it is also, and
very strongly, one of education and adaptation.

The story's plot is simple, as usual, and hinges on the familiar
love interest. A young Frenchman, orphaned since birth and
raised by the Hurons in America, arrives in France—in lower
Brittany, to be precise—where he meets a prior and his sister who
turn out to be the young man's own uncle and aunt. He is taken
into their home where he makes the acquaintance of Mlle de
St. Yves, a pretty Breton girl with whom he promptly falls in
love. Unable to marry her because of a trivial religious rule, he
sets out for Versailles to obtain special dispensation from the
King. On his way he is denounced to the authorities by a Jesuit
spy suspicious of his religious tolerance; as a result he is arrested
immediately upon his arival in Paris and locked up in the Bastille.
Through the efforts of Mlle de St. Yves he is eventually released,
a good deal wiser in the ways of the Old World. When the death
of his fiancée puts an end to his hopes of marriage, he enlists in
the army and ends up as "an excellent officer" and "an intrepid
philosopher."

Social and political criticism make their appearance from the
first. Set in 1689, during the reign of Louis XIV, the story's main
thrust is aimed at the arbitrary arrests that were common practice around that time. The Edict of Nantes had been revoked
only a few years earlier, and Louis had appointed a special minister, Monsignor de Louvois—mentioned by name in this story
—to suppress the Protestants. Persecution was savage and un-
restrained; arrests were made practically at the whim of the
oppressors. The hero undoubtedly expresses the feelings of many
an innocent victim when, terrified by the sudden loss of his
freedom, he exclaims in despair: "What! Are there then no laws
in this country? They condemn people without a hearing!" [34]

These practices had by no means ended when Voltaire wrote
The Ingénu. The Calas affair was only five years old; even fresher
in mind was the fate of the young La Barre, executed the previous year. At the time he wrote his story, the author's efforts to have
the unjustly accused Sirven family rehabilitated were in full
swing. In addition, Voltaire had his own experience of undeserved

imprisonment to draw upon. No wonder, then, that his anger against the abuses of so-called civilized society was so intense.

At first glance the indictment of society seems to outweigh all other themes. The Huron is arrested in the middle of the night, without any explanation, and conducted to prison in silence, "like a corpse that one deposits in a cemetery." [35] In his cell he meets a Jansenist by the name of Gordon, another victim of political and religious abuse. The eventual release of the pair is as arbitrary as their apprehension. It is due not to legal process, but to the beauty of Mlle de St. Yves and the corruption of the official in charge of arrests and detentions. The official's desires are aroused by the pretty girl who has come to beg him for her fiancé's freedom, and he forces her to sacrifice her virginity as the price of his services in obtaining her beloved's release. Since the heroine later dies as the consequence of her feelings of guilt and shame, she is as much a victim of the abuses of power as the two prisoners she has succeeded in liberating.

An equal share of the blame goes to the Jesuits. It is on the strength of their denunciation that the Huron and the Jansenist have been imprisoned. Indirectly, they are also responsible for the death of Mlle de St. Yves because it is a Jesuit priest, Father Tout à tous ("All Things to All Men"), who, upon learning that the man who has propositioned the innocent girl is an influential minister, persuades her with the casuistic arguments typical of his sect that it is her duty to submit.

By 1767 the Jesuit influence in France had waned considerably, but it had not completely ceased; some of their power had been taken over by the Jansenists, whose fanatical spirit dominated the French *parlements* or judicial bodies. It was the *parlement* of Toulouse that had condemned both Calas and La Barre to their unmerited deaths. Voltaire's portrayal of the Jesuits as a scheming, hypocritical, and harmful section of society could easily apply, then, to the Jansenists as well. During one of his conversations with his cell mate, the Ingénu remarks: "Your persecutors are abominable. I pity you for being oppressed, but I also pity you for being a Jansenist. All sects seem to me to be hotbeds of error." [36]

It is the relationship between the Huron and the Jansenist that gives the clearest picture of *The Ingénu's* ultimately conciliatory tone. Cut off from the rest of the world, the two find consolation in each other's presence, and the long months they spend to-

gether in captivity turn out to be profitable to both. The older
man takes it upon himself to educate the young Savage, who
may be free of prejudice but is also ignorant of the culture that
forms the basis of civilization. He instructs him in literature,
science, and philosophy, and as his intelligent and eager pupil
absorbs knowledge he imperceptibly changes from *homo naturalis*
to *homo sapiens*. Once the transformation has been completed
there is no going back, and from then on the Ingénu belongs to
Western society.

In his turn, the Huron exerts a beneficial influence on the
Jansenist, whose beliefs are frozen in the dogmas of his sect. His
logical mind never fails to spot the flaws in his mentor's reasoning, and gradually the old man abandons ideas he has never
questioned because he had never investigated them. "What!" he
reflects, "I have spent fifty years studying and I'm afraid I shall
never have the natural common sense of this almost wild boy!
I tremble at the thought of having assiduously strengthened
prejudice; he only listens to nature itself." [37]

Thus the dark prison becomes the source of enlightenment for
both inmates. By the time they regain their liberty both have
undergone a fundamental change. "The Ingénu was no longer in-
genuous," while also the Jansenist "had changed into a man, just
like the Huron." [38] Even the official responsible for the story's
love tragedy ends up feeling remorse and becomes human. It is
he who, after the death of Mlle de St. Yves, offers to make
amends to the inconsolable ex-Huron, and talks him into a military career.

"Time heals all," says Voltaire at the end of the story, stressing
the spirit of conciliation.[39] The Jansenist takes as his motto
"Misfortune is good for something," while we may be sure that
the former Ingénu, now the "intrepid philosopher," will be Voltaire's worthy follower in the forthcoming struggle for freedom." [40]

Voltaire was fond of his *Ingénu,* preferring it to *Candide*. As
he wrote to his publisher, "*The Ingénu* is better than *Candide,*
for it is infinitely more life-like." [41] Most modern readers would
quarrel with this judgment. *The Ingénu* lacks the unity of *Candide* in that it mixes satire with sentiment. Voltairian wit and
irony sparkle in the political parts of the story and in comical
scenes such as the hero's baptism, confession, and attempt at
marriage. When we switch to the trials of the heroine, however,

we are reminded of the pathos of Voltaire's drama and are close to the lachrymose. Sentimentality and social criticism do not go well together, and today readers would probably like *The Ingénu* better did not melodrama intrude into its satirical development.

The story, nevertheless, stands as a tribute to Voltaire's undiminished vigor in the fight for justice. It has been called "one of the first cannon balls hurled against the Bastille," [42] and ranks as one of the aging sage's most militant *contes*. At the same time it reflects his faith in a future in which both ignorance and prejudice will gradually yield to an increasingly enlightened humanity.

In 1767, the year in which *The Ingénu* appeared, Voltaire wrote as follows to a correspondent:

During the last fifteen years there has taken place a revolution in the minds of men which will produce a great epoch. The cries of the pedants herald this great change as the croakings of the ravens herald good weather . . . A man of my age will not see it but we will die in the hope that men may become more enlightened and more gentle. . . . What will console me when I leave the world is that I shall leave behind me a little nursery-garden of honest folk which is growing and gathering strength every day and which will end by forcing the fools and fanatics to hold their tongues. I shall not see those beautiful days but I see their dawning.[43]

Who knows whether the author of *The Ingénu* foresaw the French Revolution? He certainly predicted a period of profound change.

V *Fatalism and Atheism Revisited: Two Last* Contes

Voltaire rarely achieved in his *conte* the near-perfect fusion of form and matter, style and philosophical content that he did in his masterpiece *Candide*. Two of his very last stories, *The Story of Johnny or The Sage and the Atheist* and *Lord Chesterfield's Ears and Chaplain Goudman*, both of which appeared in 1775, illustrate how the delicate balance between idea and expression can be lost when the author loads down his story with excessive ideational content.

Both stories have their appealing points, and they are often illuminated with their author's distinctive wit and charm, but, as *contes,* as integrated works of art, they are flawed by didactic intent. The author seems to be much more interested in instructing than in pleasing, indeed, it often seems as though he is only occasionally willing to please in order to instruct. Philosophical dialogue, often running on uninterruptedly for pages and pages, sometimes seems to have been injected into the development of a story with little or no consideration as to its essential role in contributing to the story as a whole. Often the reader may forget that he is reading a *conte* by Voltaire rather than an article from his *Philosophical Dictionary.* Instead of allowing the reader to infer the moral implications of his stories, the author here, as in many of his "tearful comedies," brings home the "moral of the story" in case someone may have been so naive as to miss it. "Remember, my son, there is no happiness apart from virtue," [44] Johnny's wise father tells him when the remorseful youth has fallen upon his knees in front of him after having gone temporarily astray. And, in case the reader's mind may have wandered by the end of *Lord Chesterfield's Ears,* he is reminded one more time of "the fatality that governs all the things of this world." [45]

This explicit statement of the "moral" of the story is not in itself enough, of course, to make it fall short of Voltaire's highest level as teller of tales. In other *contes* he had sometimes moralized intentionally and with good effect. The trouble with *Lord Chesterfield's Ears* and *The Story of Johnny* lies neither in their end nor their beginning, which are appropriate (though repetitive), but in what lies between.

VI   Lord Chesterfield's Ears and Chaplain Goudman *(1775)*

The tale gets off to a good start, its narrator having made clear that he is going to relate an adventure of his that will show the omnipotence of fate over human affairs. The narrator, Chaplain Goudman, has gone to his patron Lord Chesterfield in hope of getting him to recommend him to a lucrative clerical opening of which he has heard. The deaf old nobleman, misunderstanding his request, thinks he has asked to be sent to a surgeon to be operated upon. Reverend Goudman only finds out the mistake when he ends up in the office of a surgeon, Monsieur Sidrac. While he is there, one of his competitors arrives at Lord Chesterfield's house, requests the curacy he had coveted, and receives it.

This same competitor has been able to win Goudman's mistress, Miss Fidler. Before he can make amends for his error, Lord Chesterfield dies. Disappointed in ambition and love, Goudman turns to a study of nature under the tutelage of Sidrac, as Voltaire himself once had done under the tutelage of Madame du Châtelet.

Like Voltaire, Goudman is astonished at what he observes with the aid of his senses, his spectacles, and a telescope. At times he feels as though "philosophy laughs at us." He cannot discover any trace of what was usually called nature; on the contrary, everything seems to him to be art.[46]

This sort of philosophizing continues, only in dialogue form, when Goudman, upon Sidrac's encouragement, lays aside his ambition to ever become a clergyman and decides to live henceforth on a small annuity, dine every day at Sidrac's house, and devote himself to philosophy. The chief topic that the two discuss is the nature of the soul. Their opinions turn out to be, not surprisingly, those of the author of *The Ignorant Philosopher*— Voltaire himself. They recognize that whereas in mathematics certainty might be attainable, in metaphysics nothing has been proven except one's own ignorance. Sidrac is grateful to God for this awareness that "of the principles of things I know absolutely nothing." [47]

Reflection upon God leads the two philosophers to realize that man's life is bound by necessary laws of cause and effect; the chain of cause and effect, for example, had so operated in the universe that it had been Goudman's competitor and not Goudman who had gotten the curacy and Miss Fidler. All was part of this chain of being, Sidrac informs Goudman, and God would not break it for any man, not even for Himself. This presents the thinkers with a new paradox to ponder: that "God is as much a slave as myself." "He is the slave of His will," Sidrac explains, "of His wisdom, and of the laws which He has Himself instituted; and it is impossible that He can infringe upon any of them, because it is impossible that He can become either weak or inconsistent." [48] If God, then, cannot change things in the world, why pray to Him or praise Him?, Goudman wants to know. To such questions Sidrac has no answer. "Let us do our duty to God, by being just and true to each other. In that consist our real prayers, and our most heartfelt praises." [49]

Eventually Goudman and Sidrac are joined in their metaphysical discussions by a learned physician, philosopher, and world traveler Doctor Grou, who regales them with his experiences and observations, especially of the fertility rites which he has seen practiced on the island of Tahiti with the approval of the island's queen. Later the three philosophers debate what is the prime motive in all the actions of men. Is it love and ambition, as Goudman argued? Or money, as Grou claimed? Or, as the anatomist Sidrac argued, the toilet stool? In this part of the *conte* Voltaire is well in control of his material and wit, which at times indulges in the scatological. The previous profound discussion of the soul and fate seems almost forgotten as the demands and tyranny of the flesh invade and conquer the domain of the philosophers' interest. They recognize that dysentery has sometimes changed the course of history, and constipation affected the fate of empires.

By this time the story seems to have gone far off its tracks; destiny has been forgotten for digestion, and talk has taken the place of action. At the last moment, however, the author manages to bring the story to a rollicking conclusion. Goudman's competitor has lost Miss Fidler and the curacy; Goudman is now offered the curacy in exchange for Miss Fidler by one of that lady's other admirers, a steward of Lord Chesterfield. His philosopher friends advise him to accept the offer, as with the income from the lucrative curacy he can have not only all the girls in the parish, but also Miss Fidler. The story has circled around to the point at which it began, with everyone convinced "of the fatality that governs all the things of this world." [50]

VII The Story of Johnny or The Sage and the Atheist *(1775)*

The philosophical purpose of *The Story of Johnny or The Sage and the Atheist* is to refute fanatical theology and atheistic metaphysics and to show their inferiority in theory and practice to deistic religion. Deism is represented by the pious Quaker chaplain Freind, while fanaticism is personified by the Spanish inquisitor Caracucarador and his cohort the theologian Papalamiendo, with whom Freind engages in the first of two long dialogues which interrupt the action of the story. In real life Voltaire had seen atheism advocated by Diderot, La Mettrie, and d'Holbach. In the tale it is embodied in the evil temptress

Madame Clive-Hart and her lover, the brilliant but indolent Birton, both of whom have helped lead astray the handsome, good, but weak hero of the tale, Freind's twenty-year-old son Johnny. As Birton is Johnny's mentor, Freind realizes that he must vanquish this devil-like atheist before he can redeem his son. The second of the two long dialogues consists, then, of a lengthy dialogue between the sage and the atheist.

The actual story of *The Story of Johnny* could very well have furnished material for another of Voltaire's dramas. After being rescued by his father from falling victim to Spanish inquisitors, the young Englishman Johnny has returned to England where he falls in with a fast crowd of pleasure-loving atheists. He is enchanted by Madame Clive-Hart and plunges into a life of debauchery with her and her lover Birton. Determined to win his son back to virtue, Freind finds him a suitable mate, the lovely and pure Miss Primrose, whom Johnny might have married had not the jealous Madame Clive-Hart poisoned her. After this crime the atheists escape to the New World, taking Johnny with them. Freind goes off to Maryland in search of them, and aided by friendly Indians finally succeeds in finding and liberating his son, who has been captured by an Indian tribe in the Blue Mountains. Madame Clive-Hart has been killed and scalped by the Indians. Johnny and Birton embark with Freind in a ship back to England, but only after Birton has been converted by Freind's philosophical arguments and example, and resolves to change his ways. As it turns out that Miss Primrose has made a miraculous recovery from the poisoning, Johnny, now fully returned to the path of virtue, can marry her upon his return and live happily ever after. All in all, a sentimental story that would inevitably have strong appeal for Voltaire and many of his readers.

Had Voltaire been able to curb his propagandizing impulses or even to condense his philosophizing, this *conte* might well have been one of his most successful ones. But unfortunately this was not the case. As a deist proselytizing, the author felt it was necessary to present the arguments for and against atheism in such detail, and he may have had his reasons, but a *conte* was not the place for them. In his determination to reduce everything to moral philosophy, he almost reduces a potentially good story to a slow-moving, moralistic bore. The philosophical dialogues in themselves, however, are lucid and lively, and enough sparks of the old wit still fly from the pen of the seasoned *philosophe* to make *The Story of Johnny* well worth the reader's time and attention.

CHAPTER 6

Timelessly Timely: Voltaire Today

I *Is Voltaire Obsolete?*

NO one would deny that Voltaire still occupies an important and well-deserved place in the history of ideas. Few will dispute his greatness as an historian and his genius as a satirist. At the same time, few will defend his greatness as a poet or his profundity as a philosopher. While his histories are still readable and his *contes* still enchanting, his epic and dramatic poetical works with their cardboard characters and inflated rhetoric certainly seem to have rightly been put in moth balls. But what of Voltaire the thinker? Do his ideas have any relevance to the contemporary world?

First of all, as these very questions are still lively topics for discussion, we can be assured that, whatever the final view of Voltaire's relevance more than two hundred and seventy-five years after his birth, he is not yet dead. Some, no doubt, deny that the thoughts of an eighteenth-century *philosophe* who flourished in a long-gone "age of enlightenment" can be of use to a century such as ours, with its highly complex, rapidly developing technological societies. What did Voltaire know of computers, atomic fission, DNA, test-tube babies, behavioral engineering, space satellites, and future shock? His stories may still be gems, but his ideas are fossils.

But are they?

We don't think so. And we are not alone.

In this concluding chapter we will briefly refer to seven areas in which, we believe, Voltaire still has something of value to relate to twentieth-century men and women. Not that our list is intended to be exhaustive. Far from it. Had space permitted, we would have liked to have considered Voltaire's relevance to education, to ecology, to science fiction, to occultism, to rites of passage, and so on. But brief as our discussion of Voltaire's topicality must be, it will suggest, we hope, why the Voltairian, an endangered species in the world today, is not yet extinct.

Voltairian? Here is one of the best definitions of the species that we have come across.

A Voltairian is a man who is bent on seeing clearly in all matters; in religion and philosophy he is willing to believe only that which he understands, and to accept ignorance in all the rest; he values reality more than speculation, and simplifies ethics as well as dogma, both for the sake of practical virtues; in politics he favors a moderation that guarantees natural freedom, as well as the freedoms of conscience, of expression, and of person; one which eliminates as much evil and brings about as much good as possible, and places justice among the most desirable goods; in the arts he appreciates restraint and truth above all; he hates hypocrisy, fanaticism and bad taste with a passion and, not limiting himself to hating these, he will fight them to the bitter end.[1]

II Bridging the Two Cultures: "Poet and Physicist"

One way in which Voltaire remains relevant to our own times lies in his awareness of the need for attaining, through education, a perspective on life that bridges the gap between what C. P. Snow calls the "two cultures"—the humanities and the sciences.[2] An artist by inclination and talent, he undertook the arduous task of reeducating himself in his maturity, immersing himself in the science and philosophy of his day until he could understand and articulate the "new language" of Locke, Leibniz, and Newton. He was proud to think of himself as both a poet *and* a physicist. At least up until the middle of his century he kept up with the latest philosophical and scientific ideas, writing lucid popularizations of them in order to spread far and wide the gospel of enlightment. For a while he even engaged in scientific experiments—on fire and motive forces. Although these remained strictly in the amateur class, they revealed the extent of his commitment to applying scientific methods to the discovery of new truths. Thus he provided a model for his large readership to emulate in their search for knowledge. Margaret Sherwood Libby in her study *The Attitude of Voltaire to Magic and the Sciences* refers to him as a "philosophical journalist" who was interested in doing more than merely gathering material from others in order to write readable books.[3] The breadth of his interest, his determination to formulate for himself the new theories, to assimilate and evaluate them, made him more than a mere popularizer. As Libby writes,

He seemed above all an ardent student, a perpetual undergraduate, whose university was the Europe of the eighteenth century, whose professors were the great men of his time, one who took many courses, refused to specialize to any extent and wrote exercises and essays partly for sheer enjoyment and desire to excel, partly to fix the information in his own mind.[4]

After the middle of the century Voltaire all but abandoned his attempt to stay abreast of new developments in the sciences. He became far more interested in launching his concerted attack on the "infamy" of religious bigotry in which he used as ammunition whatever scientific and philosophical ideas he had previously acquired that might suit his purpose. Nevertheless, he remained throughout his life a remarkably well informed and broadly educated man, a true generalist. He certainly would have agreed with Snow that a person lacking a knowledge and appreciation of scientific culture, no matter how well educated he may be in the humanities, is impoverished and only half educated. He would, at the same time, have considered as uncouth a scientist who had no training in the humanities and lacked a poetic imagination. Voltaire saw no reason why "the study of physics should crush the flowers of poetry." [5] And he was equally convinced that the study of poetry would not spoil the fruit of scientific investigation.

In our age of fragmentation and specialization the example of Voltaire as a mind that bridged the two cultures can be salutary. Someone has said that a person has two educations, the one he is given and the one he gives himself. The Jesuits provided Voltaire with the first; for the second, he was his own tutor. True offspring of the enlightenment, he left behind his reliance upon the tutelage of others to think and to learn for himself. His was truly a liberal education, encompassing ultimately the totality of reality. Voltaire, educator, still has much to teach us.

III   *"Philosophe, Heal Thyself!": Therapist Voltaire*

I have studied medicine as Madame Pimbesche learned legal customs
—in pleading; I have read Sydenham, Freind, Boerhaave. I know
that this art can only be a conjectural one . . . I have concluded that
one must be one's own doctor, live on a careful diet, aid nature from
time to time, never force her, but above all know how to suffer, grow
old, and die.[6]

The attitude toward life and toward the art by which it may
be sustained, expressed by Voltaire in the above passage from
one of his letters to a physician, suggests another reason why he
is still timely today. Throughout his long, eventful, and often
traumatic life, he developed a practical philosophy that made
it possible for him to face crises, to adjust to change, and to
continue to live on productively for more than seven decades.
The attitude toward life and death that sprang from this philosophy and some of the insights that supported it still have value
and relevance to contemporary readers.
    First and foremost, he followed Epicurus in drawing attention
to the importance of health as the basis for all goods, material as
well as mental. It quickly becomes obvious to all readers of
Voltaire's letters that he was always concerned, usually over-
concerned, about his health. Although he undoubtedly had
several real ailments, he was in fact a confirmed hypochondriac.
From his youth, when he shrank from excesses which might have
damaged his fragile health, to his old age, when he complained
to his physician that he was crushed by "eighty-four years and
eighty-four maladies," physical well-being was to him of paramount importance.[7] In itself, nothing about all this is unique or
laudable, but the objectivity and sensitivity with which Voltaire
was able to view his own (and his friends') physical condition
was unusual, and the advice that he gave was often remarkably
sensible.
    Basically Voltaire's way to *ataraxia*—absence of pain in the
body and mind—was to cooperate rather than to interfere with
nature. Cleanliness, exercise, simple and healthful diet, and
avoidance of extremes were among his most frequent recommen-
dations. "What medicine will make you digest? Exercise. What
will regain your strength? Sleep. What will diminish your in-
curable ills? Patience."[8] Such was his advice. Medicine, as he

stated in his *Philosophical Dictionary,* is basically "clearing up, cleaning up, and keeping up the house that one cannot rebuild." [9] Like all arts, it consists, he held, of doing what is appropriate.

The proper nourishment and care of the body must be accompanied by attitudes, habits, and conceptions conducive to the attainment and maintenance of an enlightened mind. Like Epicurus, Voltaire held that fear of death is one of the chief obstacles to enlightened happiness, and he was equally determined to overcome it. His attempt to do this is most evident in his letters to his lifetime friend, Mme du Deffand, who, after having become blind, was often subject to fits of deep depression during which she questioned the value of living and expressed her fear of dying to her friends, most of all to Voltaire. In responding to his old friend's pessimistic reflections, he formulated clearly the life-affirming philosophy by which he lived and by which he himself would eventually die. In a typical passage from one of these letters, he wrote:

I think, everything considered, we should never think of death: the thought is good for nothing except to poison life. The main thing is not to suffer; as for the moment of death, it's as insensible as the moment of sleep. The people who announce it ceremoniously are the enemies of the human race; we must prevent them from ever getting close to us. Death is nothing at all; only the idea is sad. Therefore, let's never think of it, and live from day to day. Let's get up each morning saying: What shall I do today for my health and amusement? At our age everything comes down to just that.[10]

Thus, for Voltaire, as for Epicurus, death itself is nothing of great importance. So long as we live we have experiences through our sense organs, but at death these sense organs cease to operate and we can therefore experience nothing at all. Why fear nothing? But along with his Epicurean rejection of the fear of death, Voltaire maintained a stoical resignation to it, which was an offspring, perhaps, of his confirmed belief in scientific determinism. As he formulated it in another letter to Mme du Deffand:

This is, perhaps, madam, what I would suggest as a remedy . . . You couldn't help but write the very philosophic and very sad letter that I received from you; and I am writing to you, of necessity, that courage, resignation to nature's laws, profound disdain for all forms of superstition, the superior pleasure of knowing oneself to be of a different kind from fools, and the exercise of the faculty of reason are true consolations.[11]

This was the belief by which Voltaire supported his everyday life into the ripeness of old age while he calmly awaited the dissolution of his being. To him, as to Spinoza, philosophy was a meditation not on death but on life. Long before Bertrand Russell, but in strikingly similar terms, he formulated his own "free man's worship." In our day, Voltaire's clear-headed and tenacious affirmation of the value of life can offer refreshment to those who, like Mme du Deffand, still feel that it is a misfortune to be born, and that the remedy of the misfortune—death—is even worse than the disease.

IV   Knowing that One Does Not Know: A True Disbeliever

We are, of course, an ignorant lot; even the best of us knows how to do only a few things well; and of what is available in knowledge of fact, whether of science or of history, only the smallest part is in any one man's knowing.[12]

This statement could very well have been taken from Voltaire's work, The Ignorant Philosopher. The author is, however, one of the great scientists of the twentieth century, J. Robert Oppenheimer. The sceptical spirit, so strong in Voltaire, is another of the features of his thought that seems useful to our age of rapid and unpredictable change, proliferation of novelty, and impending "future shock." It might also provide a counterfoil to the wide variety of contemporary dogmas and cults that are sometimes adjoined to fanatical proselytizing and violence. Although in Voltaire doubting is never absolute—he does, of course, accept as provable at least God, gravity, and geometry—it was an attitude of mind that helped him, as it might help us, to cope with stress and to adjust to the unexpected.

For Voltaire's ignorant philosopher, as for Socrates, philosophy was only a refined sense of one's own ignorance. For his Good Brahmin, ignorance had grown rather than diminished with the passing years, humbling him and at times making life seem nearly unbearable. As he, Job-like, exclaims,

I was born, I live in time, and I do not know what time is; I find my-self in a point between two eternities . . . and I have no idea of eternity; I am made up of matter, I think, I have never been able to discover what it is that produces thought . . . Not only the origin of my thoughts is unknown to me, but the origin of my movements is equally hidden. I do not know why I exist . . . I am ready sometimes to fall into despair when I think that after all my studies I do not know where I come from, nor who I am, nor where I am going, nor what I shall become.[13]

While this passage is characteristic of Voltaire's scepticism in its Pascalian mood, it totally lacks the scathing wit and mocking humor so often associated with his doubting. The giant Micro-mégas's conversation with the earthling philosophers is a good case in point.[14] His admiration for the tiny but apparently ra-tional beings turns to disgust and indignation when they describe their habitual squabbling in time of peace and purposeless slaughtering in time of war. The giant's impulse (which he only with difficulty checks) is to take a few steps and stamp out "this whole anthill of ridiculous assassins."

Bertrand Russell, incidentally, finds this passage from *Micro-mégas* even more tragically appropriate in our century than when it was written more than two hundred years ago.[15] In describing the influence that Voltaire had upon his own thinking, Russell points out that he had learned to agree with the *philosophe's* belief that no opinion should be held with fervor. "When a man holds some opinion with immense fervor, and you believe this opinion to be false," Russell writes, "you should not—so I think Voltaire held—endeavor to cause the opposite opinion to be held with fervor." [16] If you can know something to be the case, for example, that seven times eight is fifty-six, you don't hold it with fervor, Russell argues. Only doubtful or demonstrably false opinions are usually asserted with fervor. Russell believes that it is the excess of moral fervor that provides the impetus to violence and war. For when two competing sides are equally fervent in their convictions that they, and they alone, are right, ferocious feelings are triggered and violence erupts. In place of this irrational and troublesome emotion, Russell, fol-lowing Voltaire, would put scepticism and ridicule. Ridicule, he holds, is quite an appropriate and powerful weapon to use against dogmatists who preach doctrines as absolutely certain, when a confession of ignorance would be more rational and more honest.[17] With Voltaire he would advise, "Laugh and you shall crush them."

Today's "true disbelievers" continue, in the spirit of Voltaire, and for much the same reasons, to use ridicule as a weapon against fanatical "true believers." Even though they themselves are doubtful they can know anything with absolute certainty, Voltairians, like their model and like Socrates, at least believe that others are far less wise than they when these nonsceptics claim not only to know the absolute truth, but to have an absolute monopoly on it. At least the Voltairians can allow themselves the satisfaction of deflating these dangerous windbags with the sharp pricks of their scepticism and ridicule.

V Watching a World Go Madder: Comic Genius

If Voltaire lives on today, it is, for the great majority of his readers, because of his sense of humor. Like Aristophanes and Mark Twain, he was one of the world's great comic geniuses. Along with his support of the more traditional human freedoms he also supported one equally important, the freedom to laugh. Laughter was, for him, as we have already pointed out, a powerful weapon in everyman's fight for liberation from the forces of fanaticism, intolerance, and tyranny. "Laugh, and you shall crush them," was his advice to the dissatisfied, the repressed, and the exploited. And while he lived, the rich and powerful feared the torrent of laughter that could be directed against them by a flick of his pen, the most deadly weapon that he wielded.

But even when Voltaire was most engaged as a writer he was not always diabolical with the humorous weapons of which he was a master. He recognized that laughter could also relieve boredom, alleviate pain, and reconcile men, at least for the moment, to the facts of life and death. For, after all, while laughter could be precipitated by human foibles it was quite natural for humans to laugh as a simple expression of joy. "Laughter always arises from a gaiety of disposition absolutely incompatible with contempt and indignation," he once wrote.[18] This would leave out the laughter of ridicule of which he was a past master. Although Voltaire never dealt with the aesthetics of comedy to the extent that he did with that of tragedy, his practice shows that he had many strings on his comic lyre, and the range of his comic devices were as wide as they were varied. Here we can only mention a few.[19]

Voltaire was capable of Rabelaisian buffoonery (e.g., in his mock-epic on Joan of Arc, *La Pucelle*) and of Swiftian irony (e.g., *Micromégas*). He could compose an aphorism as coldly witty and as devastatingly cutting as La Rochefoucauld (e.g., "To forgive our enemies their virtues—that is a greater miracle"). He could also formulate a paradox as memorable as any by his later imitator Oscar Wilde: "The multitude of books is making us ignorant." Like Aristophanes he recognized fully the manifold humor in the relations between the sexes (e.g., "God created women only to tame men"). Long before Mark Twain, he was using wit to suggest man's gross inhumanity to man (e.g., "The punishment of criminals should be of use; when a man is hanged he is good for nothing"). He sounds to us at times like an eighteenth-century Will Rogers: "The art of government consists in taking as much money as possible from one class of citizens to give to the other." At other times he reveals himself as the true precursor of H.L. Mencken: "In the great game of human life one begins by being a dupe and ends up by being a rogue."

Even though Voltaire said little about why he chose the devices he did to achieve the effects he intended, his practice was so consistent that one can usually infer the principles by which his humor and wit operated. Sometimes his comic effect springs from an implied sense of superiority, as when he, the refined French gourmet, states that "England has forty-two religions and two sauces." Sometimes he achieves the effect by sardonic incongruity: "I knew I was among civilized men because they were fighting so savagely." He is also capable of achieving comic effects by releasing inhibitions about sexual relationships, as when he writes: "The husband who desires to surprise is often very much surprised himself." His range of comic devices included exaggeration (e.g., "The fate of a nation has often depended upon the good or bad digestion of a prime minister") and understatement (e.g., "Common sense is not so common"). He exploited fully both irony of expression (e.g., "A clergyman is one who feels himself called upon to live without working at the expense of radicals who work to live") and irony of situation ("I was never ruined but twice: once when I lost a lawsuit, and once when I won one"). His writings are liberally sprinkled with wisecracks such as "A woman can keep one secret—her age" and epigrams (e.g., "When it is a question of money, everybody is of the same religion"). He resorts to riddles and clever repartee in his *contes*. When Zadig is asked "What is the thing that we receive without giving thanks, enjoy without knowing how, give to others when we don't know where we are, and lose without knowing it," he replies "Life." [20] When Cacambo asks Candide, "What is optimism?", Candide replies: "Alas, it is the mania of maintaining that all is well when we are miserable!" [21] Even Voltaire's *Philosophical Dictionary* has sometimes been considered to be a sophisticated jokebook.

Voltaire is at his best, however, when he is not just being funny but when he is hurling the thunderbolts of his wit to chastise a villain or to fell an enemy. Then he can be ruthless, devastating, lethal. One has only to recall the effect his *Diatribe of Doctor Akakia* had upon Maupertuis as an example of the effectiveness of his brilliant and sometimes cruel wit. When he finally disappeared from the eighteenth-century scene, it can truly be said that he was sorely missed. For, as two contemporary historians have pointed out, "for sixty years this sparkling little Frenchman bestrode Europe like a Colossus, lashing fools with his sarcasm, pouring acid on bigots, fighting obscurantism with unmatched irony." [22]

Suppose Voltaire were to come back to earth today. Would he find equally tempting targets to attack with his satirical pen? Our modern world would indeed offer him abundant material for a new *Candide, Micromégas,* or *Philosophical Dictionary.* The spectacle of great powers stockpiling atomic weapons in order to assure peace would certainly horrify him. A recent war, supposedly waged to protect a foreign people but which ended by virtually destroying that people's land, would send him into peals of shrill laughter. The development of nations which in the name of freedom, progress, and peace continually and brutally repress their artists and writers would drive him to further satiric fury, and link him to such modern satirists as Eugene Zamiatin and George Orwell. Scathing irony would also be Voltaire's response to our suicidal destruction of the world's natural resources under the guise of development. With what painful surprise would he note the fatal contrast between our gigantic technological advances and the total lack of our ethical growth! He would surely say, with his fellow playwright Beaumarchais, that "I hasten to laugh at everything, for fear of being obliged to weep." Grim laughter indeed would be his response to a world which, long after the warning of *Candide*, has grown only madder, and become bloodier than the eighteenth century could ever have dreamed of.

"We still need, as in Voltaire's time," writes George R. Havens, "to learn how to ridicule and laugh out of court all the host of intolerable abuses which beset us." [23]

VI *Grating Incongruities: Analyst of the Absurd*

Voltaire's highly developed sense of the absurd is another of his characteristics that make him still relevant to a century in which "The Absurd" has become a major aesthetic category. "Absurd," as the contemporary playwright Eugène Ionesco sees it, "is that which is devoid of purpose . . . Cut off from his religious, metaphysical, and transcendental roots, man is lost; all his actions become senseless, absurd, useless." [24] Ionesco and other practitioners of the Theatre of the Absurd, unlike philosophers, do not argue in the abstract; they present the human condition concretely upon the stage as they see it, with all its contradictions and incongruities. Voltaire did precisely the same in *Candide*. There, he presented an absurd world of which man tries, in vain, to make sense. The glaring contradiction between expectation and reality, between ideal and fact, awakens in the reader mixed feelings of outrage and amusement corresponding to those of the author.

Martin Esslin correctly said of the Theatre of the Absurd that it "transcends the categories of comedy and tragedy and combines laughter with horror." [25] We might say the same of *Candide*, for in it Voltaire, like Bertold Brecht later, administers a kind of shock therapy which achieves an "alienation effect." The reader does not identify with the characters but assumes a cool, objective attitude, as does Candide at the end, when he says, "that's all very well said, but in the meantime we must cultivate our garden."

From a somewhat different perspective, Albert Camus in *The Myth of Sisyphus* finds the basis of the absurd in "that divorce between the mind that desires and the world that disappoints, my nostalgia for unity, this fragmented universe and the contradiction that binds them together." [26] The "Myth of Candide" created by Voltaire is a perfect illustration of this perspective, for what else is his hero but the personification of the precarious human balancing act between fact and fiction? A contemporary Voltairian scholar, Patrick Henry, in a study of Voltaire and Camus on the absurd, has shown how both "realized that reason would never fathom metaphysics or the problems of evil and human destiny." [27] Yet both thinkers refused to renounce reason and take the leap of faith which might have resolved the contradictions they faced. Comparing Candide with Meursault in Camus' *Stranger,* Henry sees both heroes as strangers to other men and to themselves.[28] Eventually both break through their habitual illusions and reach a higher level of self-consciousness and individuality. Neither commits suicide, although, in Henry's view, Candide's teacher Dr. Pangloss commits "philosophical suicide" by his unswerving adherence to optimism. Meursault lives without hope and dies happy. Candide lives on, but after renouncing all hope of achieving a perfect love or a perfect society. "Voltaire maintains the absurd paradox," Henry concludes, "proclaiming the absurd on the one hand and elevating life on the other." [29]

In a similar view, other commentators have seen in Candide, and even in Zadig, paradigms of the committed existentialist hero. Thomas C. Greening sees Candide as "the peer of Camus' Sisyphus in his progress from naive optimism and passive vulnerability" to a freely chosen task.[30] Greening extols Candide for taking a stand and thereby committing himself, simultaneously affirming his imprisonment in the world and his freedom. Voltaire's Zadig also has his contemporary admirers who make him out to be a hero of the absurd. "In his role as exemplary hero," writes George A. Perla, "Zadig must pass through the stages of credulity, doubt, and despair, and shed his naive assumptions before he can discover within himself a unifying principle which will free him for a purposive existence and beneficial action upon the world." [31]

Whether or not all this is reading too much into Voltaire's characters and *contes,* it at least makes clear that Voltaire's art still speaks to us.

VII   *Beyond Utopia/Dystopia: Voltaire, Meliorist*

Today Voltaire recommends himself to those who, while rejecting the possibility of ever achieving a utopia, nevertheless continue to work for a better world. Voltaire remains a critic of utopias and a mentor of meliorists. Imaginary societies may offer aesthetic gratification and psychological balm, but there seems little chance of their ever becoming functional realities. Instead of wasting our time longing for a non-existing paradise, we had better turn our attention to improving conditions as they are. "The best," in Voltaire's opinion, "is the enemy of the good." Like Henry David Thoreau, he believed he came into the world not to make it into a perfect place in which to live, but to live in it. "The terrestrial paradise is where I am," he summed up his viewpoint in *The Man of the World.* Far better to own one chateau at Ferney than a dozen castles in Eldorado. The message of *Candide* is also the message of Voltaire's entire life: don't rationalize, but work; don't utopianize, but improve. We must cultivate our own garden, for no one is going to do it for us.

Nor has this enlightened horticulture become outmoded. A recent commentator, Merle L. Perkins, for example, considers Voltaire's concept of international order far from fossilized today.[32] And some of his ideas on war and peace, Perkins argues, are still quite sound and relevant:

In our own day, if there has been partial success in establishing new institutions as the means of peace, it can accurately be said that they are dependent on some of the conditions which Voltaire saw as prerequisite: reduction of distrust and superstition among peoples; the elevation of diplomacy above the Machiavellian tradition; redefinition of concepts of sovereignty to stress defense more than aggrandizement.[33]

Henry Meyer, another scholar who agrees with Perkins on the contemporaneousness of Voltaire's thought, has shown how Voltaire, the peace-loving *philosophe,* was far in advance of his time (and, in some respects, of ours) in denouncing war, in deploring its destruction of life and property, and in probing its origins in human nature and history.[34] Voltaire may not have hit on solutions to our common problems, nor did he propose plans for infallible peace as did his contemporary, the Abbé de St. Pierre, but he did ask the right questions and he suggested the direction in which we might be able to find some answers.

Voltaire the meliorist always rejected simple answers to complex questions. In the social scientist Karl Popper's terminology, he was an advocate of piecemeal rather than total utopian planning. He had seen the harm done when fanatics, seizing on an idea, no matter how untenable, sought to force it on their fellow creatures. He detested the presumption that lay behind the efforts of those who claimed to have the absolute truth in politics, religion, or ethics through some higher source. Like Popper, he saw a connection between utopian dreams and violence, for "true believers" must rely on coercion in order to promote their schemes.[35] (*Mohammed* was his description of such a type.) It was better, in his view, to have humanity struggling slowly toward the light than to have it deceived into thinking that a well-run but un-free society was the "best of all possible worlds."

Man is to be saved not by faith, but by works. "My greatest work," Voltaire said in one of his last poems, "is that I have done a little good." [36] We may never be able to make a utopian world, but we can at least try to make the world we live in a little less dystopian.

VIII   *Renewing the Rights of Man: Symbol of Liberty*

"His spirit still torments the world like a fever and like a reproach." [37] This statement by Paul Chaponnière about Voltaire's continuing influence highlights yet another reason why Voltaire remains a potent force. For he stood for justice, and justice still does not prevail today. Although he never gave a clear, all-encompassing definition of justice, Voltaire insisted that it could never exist so long as the essential dignity of man was not respected and men were not free—free to believe what they wished and to live according to these beliefs, free to be secure in their possessions and persons, so long as they did not disturb others. "What does it mean to be free?" Voltaire asked. "It means to reason correctly, to know the rights of man; and when they are well known, they are well defended." [38]

Voltaire's words would be echoed in the "Declaration of the Rights of Man" in 1789 after the leaders of the French Revolution had begun to put the *philosophe's* precepts into effect. As Renée

Waldinger and others have stated, Voltaire himself may not have foreseen the coming revolution, which his ideas probably helped to bring about, but nevertheless its creators widely considered him to be its prophet and their mentor.[39] One of them said of Voltaire in 1791, while the revolution was in full swing, that "his penetrating vision read into the future and saw the dawn of freedom, of that regeneration of France the seeds of which he sowed with equal zeal and courage." [40]

The spirit of Voltaire has, in fact, tended to be identified with the spirit of revolution. To some, knowing the poet's contempt for the "rabble" and his liking for benevolent despots, this itself is highly ironic. After the French Revolution, the fervor over Voltaire, defender of the Rights of Man, gradually diminished, and as the political climate changed, his name was associated with other causes. Yet as Heinrich Heine wrote, "in the liberation war of humanity, Voltaire's name will be forever memorable." [41]

In the twentieth century the name of Voltaire again reached its apogee in 1944, with the liberation of France from Nazi domination.[42] All at once the smiling sage of Ferney became for many people in France and in the Soviet Union "the symbol of liberty." While some French critics found Voltaire irrelevant to the times, he was widely hailed by others as "the prototype of writers of the Resistance." [43] Representatives of the freed French nation joined together to celebrate the 250th anniversary of his birth. And as one of his admirers remarked, Voltaire had never seemed younger. "To love Voltaire," another of them, Emile Henriot, proclaimed, "is to reject automatism, intolerance, and deception; it is to venerate intelligence; it is to know when it is necessary to say 'No'; above all, it is to love France." [44] After long years of purges and pogroms, dictators and death camps, mass warfare and saturation bombing, Voltaire's spirit—the spirit of clarity, reasonableness, justice, and love of life—was seen as a deintoxicating, restorative force, not only for Frenchmen, but for all mankind.

More recently, when a President of the United States pronounced that "our moral sense dictates our clear-cut preference for those societies which share with us an abiding respect for individual human rights," [45] his words clearly reflected the Voltairian spirit. It still represents a beacon to those who long for freedom as well as a strong reproach for those who deny toleration and justice to others. As the President put it, "because we are free we can never be indifferent to the fate of freedom elsewhere." [46] Voltaire could not have agreed with him more. And, we might add, because we are free, we can never be indifferent to Voltaire. Will and Ariel Durant even went so far as to conclude in their *Age of Voltaire* that "when we cease to honor Voltaire we shall be unworthy of freedom." [47]

What relevance Voltaire will have to readers of the future is for them, not for us, to determine. But what Paul Valéry said shortly after France's liberation in 1944 still seems true today: "Voltaire lives, Voltaire endures; he is timelessly timely" *(indéfiniment actuel).*[48]

IX   Conclusion: The Man in the Ironic Mask

For reasons set forth, then, Voltaire remains a lively, continuing influence upon our time. If he had not existed, we would have had to invent him. One of his contemporaries visiting the seventy-year-old philosopher at Ferney found him even then to be "too great to be contained within the limits of his country," and called him "a present that nature has given to the whole world." [49] We need Voltaire today, as the world has always needed him, for what, in the words of Gustave Lanson, he was: "a procedure, a method of education, a philosophy of life." [50] The procedure was sceptical; the method of education, scientific; the philosophy of life, humanistic.

A modern biochemist, Harold J. Morowitz, recently pointed to "a fundamental flaw in our educational system" that renders young people so vulnerable to irrational movements: the omissions from school curricula of "training in methods of establishing the validity of ideas." [51] By failing to teach students critical thinking, Morowitz believes, "we leave them easy prey to cult leaders, charismatic politicians and other less bizarre irrationalism such as food fads." [52] As a guideline to such critical thinking, Voltaire's works can continue to play an important role in present-day society.

Finally, Voltaire remains a subject of interest and controversy for one last reason. No one, not even the lifelong Voltaire scholar, has ever succeeded in totally comprehending the man or in completely unmasking him. What was Voltaire really like? Who was the genuine man behind the ironic mask? What was the meaning of that unforgettable smile which the 18th century

French sculptor Houdon, among others, immortalized? Was it the enlightened smile of the Buddha? The compassionate smile of a Socrates? The sceptical smile of a Montaigne? Perhaps all of these at the same time, blending into the unique, characteristic smile of that particular and peculiar man, Voltaire. Even with the ample materials available, no one can ever penetrate the real Voltaire because we must always recreate him in our own image, in the light of our own times, and each age gets the Voltaire it needs and deserves. As William Blake recognized, life is always "a fiction . . . made up of contradiction."

No one certainly was more contradictory than Voltaire. A staunch defender of truth, he was at the same time one of the world's consummate masters of the art of lying. He was a symbol of liberty who did not believe in free will; a religious sceptic who refused to doubt the existence of God; an experimentalist whose "passions dictated his conclusions." [53] He was a powerful proponent of toleration for everyone's ideas except those who attacked his own; a lover of humanity who hounded to death those whom he loathed; a savior who refused to be crucified. Courageous and cowardly, affectionate and suspicious, original and conforming, sincere and hypocritical, rational and impulsive, an Apollonian and a Dionysian—Voltaire was all this, and more. "He is amoral, violent, a thief, jealous, petty," says André Delattre in *Voltaire, L'impétueux*, "but he has, nevertheless, moral grandeur, a healthy heart, an affectionate, good, and generous nature." [54] Few have wished to defend his character in detail, yet, as Delattre points out, few have found it possible to condemn it as a whole. For, after all, Voltaire was only human, and perhaps only a little less imperfect than even the best of his species.

The final word on Voltaire will never be spoken. Perhaps, as Paul Valéry suggested, he was such a versatile human being that only music could follow him. "That devil of a man, whose mobility, resources, and contradictions make him a person that music alone, the most lively music, could follow." [55]

Our last word is to remind the reader that Voltaire, first and last, always thought of himself as a moralist. "Everything must be reduced to moral philosophy," he stressed.[56] He was a moralist not in the tradition of Moses, Mohammed, and Jesus, but in the tradition of Socrates, Confucius, and Bertrand Russell. His was a moral philosophy that emphasized perpetual inquisi-

tiveness and utility, and decried egoism and fanatical zeal. He
pronounced no set of laws which supposedly had divine sanction.
He encouraged no sense of guilt nor demanded expiation of sins.
He claimed no inspiration of a god for his beliefs, collected no
followers or disciples, fomented no holy wars, and initiated no
utopian experiments. Above all, he wanted no martyrs to sacrifice
themselves for his cause. He stood primarily for one thing:
sanity. His was a sanity of reason, of mutual aid, of tolerance, of
peace, and of moderation in all things—even, as the Chinese
would insist, in moderation.

Voltaire had reason to smile. His universe was governed not
only by gravity but by levity. The moralist behind the mask
loved to live—and to laugh.

Notes and References

Chapter One

1. The following account of the life of Voltaire is based mainly on his Correspondence, the earlier lives by Condorcet and Gustave Desnoiresterres, and the later biographies such as those by Theodore Besterman and Alfred O. Aldridge. (See Bibliography.)

2. Norman L. Torrey, *The Spirit of Voltaire* (New York: Columbia University Press, 1938), p. 1.

3. On Voltaire's health see L. J. Moorman, "Tuberculosis and Genius: Voltaire," *Annals of Medical History,* New Series, Vol. III (1931).

4. The poet was Rochebrune. See Theodore Besterman, *Voltaire* (New York: Harcourt, Brace & World, 1969), pp. 20–22.

5. On Voltaire's friends at Louis-le-Grand, see Besterman, *Voltaire,* pp. 38–41.

6. So called because they met at the previous French headquarters of the Knights Templar.

7. See Alfred O. Aldridge, *Voltaire and the Century of Light* (Princeton: Princeton University Press, 1975), p. 14.

8. Theodore Besterman (ed.), *Voltaire's Correspondence* (Geneva: Institut et Musée Voltaire, 1953–1965), 3487 (15 October 1749). Hereafter abbreviated Best., *Corres.* with number of letter and date. Unless otherwise specified, translations in the text are ours.

9. The critic was La Motte. See Aldridge, *Voltaire and the Century of Light,* p. 21.

10. On Voltaire's change of name see Ira O. Wade, "Voltaire's Name," *PMLA* 44 (1929), pp. 546–64. Among the explanations proposed are that the name is derived from an anagram of *Arouet le jeune,* the name of a family estate, the phrase *"Je vole ma terre,"* an Italian town (Volterra), a nickname (*"Le volontaire"*), a French town (Airvault), a juxtaposition of *Volaterrae* and *Arretium,* and a character (Voltare) in a play by Jobert.

11. Voltaire, *Works* (translated by William F. Fleming and others) (New York: The St. Hubert Guild, 1901), Vol. VIII, Pt. II, p. 187. Hereafter abbreviated Voltaire, *Works* (Fleming trans.).

12. See Besterman, *Voltaire,* pp. 91–92.

13. Voltaire, *Oeuvres complètes,* ed. Louis Moland (Paris: Garnier,

1877–1885), Vol. 22, pp. 18–19. Hereafter abbreviated Moland, followed by volume and page numbers.

14. Richard A. Brooks, *The Selected Letters of Voltaire* (New York: New York University Press, 1973), p. 26.

15. Voltaire, quoted in Gavin de Beer, "Voltaire's British Visitors," *Studies on Voltaire and the Eighteenth Century* (Geneva: Institut et Musée Voltaire, 1957), 4, p. 108. Henceforth abbreviated *SVEC*.

16. Archibald Ballantyne, *Voltaire's Visit to England, 1726–1729* (Geneva: Slatkine Reprints, 1970), p. 148.

17. Voltaire, quoted in John Morgan, *Journal* (Philadelphia, 1907) in Aldridge, *Voltaire and the Century of Light*, p. 315.

18. On this period of Voltaire's life see Nancy Mitford, *Voltaire in Love* (New York: Harper & Row, 1957).

19. President Henault, quoted in Mitford, *Voltaire in Love*, p. 194.

20. See Ira O. Wade, *Voltaire and Madame du Châtelet, an Essay on the Intellectual Activity at Cirey* (Princeton: Princeton University Press, 1941).

21. For estimates of Madame du Châtelet's intellectual endowments see Mitford, *Voltaire in Love*, p. 79–80, Besterman, *Voltaire*, pp. 183–84, and Ira O. Wade, *The Intellectual Development of Voltaire* (Princeton: Princeton University Press, 1969), pp. 265–77. Hereafter cited as Wade, *Intellectual Development*.

22. Best., *Corres.* 1272 (27 May 1737).

23. Aldridge, *Voltaire and the Century of Light*, p. 171.

24. See Wade, *Intellectual Development*, p. 253.

25. See Ira O. Wade, *Voltaire and Madame du Châtelet*, Conclusion.

26. R. A. Brooks (ed.), *Selected Letters of Voltaire*, p. 125, p. 152.

27. Best., *Corres.* 3487 (15 October 1749).

28. Best., *Corres.* 3474 (13 September 1749).

29. Thomas Carlyle, *History of Friedrich II of Prussia Called Frederick the Great* (New York: Scribner, Welford & Company, 1873), Vol. VI, p. 196. See also C. P. Gooch, *Frederick the Great* (Hamden, Conn., Archon Books, 1962), Chaps. VII–IX.

30. Best., *Corres.* 4335 (24 July 1752).

31. Best., *Corres.* 3978 (2 September 1751).

32. Best., *Corres.* 3617 (14 August 1750).

33. Ibid., 4486 (18 December 1752).

34. Best., *Corres.* 4418 (15 October 1752).

35. Voltaire, quoted in Aldridge, *Voltaire and the Century of Light*, p. 218.

36. Best., *Corres.* 6282 (9 August 1756).

37. R. A. Brooks, *Selected Letters of Voltaire*, p. 179.

38. See Fernand Caussy, *Voltaire, seigneur de village* (Paris: Hachette, 1912.

39. Boufflers, quoted in Aldridge, *Voltaire and the Century of Light,* p. 313.

40. Theodore Besterman, *Voltaire,* p. 533.

41. Best., *Corres.* 4855 (2 September 1753).

42. See Burdette Kinne, "Voltaire never said it!", *Modern Language Notes* 58 (1943), pp. 534–35. This recounts that S. G. Tallentyre (Mrs. Evelyn Hall), a biographer of Voltaire, not Voltaire himself was the source of the famous line "I disapprove of what you say, but I will defend to the death your right to say it."

43. Besterman, *Voltaire,* p. 517.

44. See Aldridge, *Voltaire and the Century of Light,* pp. 399–400.

45. Best., *Corres.* D17125 (5 April 1771).

46. R. A. Brooks, *Selected Letters of Voltaire,* p. 313.

47. Best., *Corres.* Vol. 129, Appendix D95, p. 357.

48. See René Pomeau's account in his Commentary on Gustave Lanson, *Voltaire,* translated by Robert A. Wagoner (New York: John Wiley & Sons, 1960), pp. 193–95.

49. Quoted in Marius Roustan, *The Pioneers of the French Revolution* (London: Ernest Benn, 1926), p. 294.

Chapter Two

1. Voltaire, *Works* (Fleming trans.), Vol. VI, Pt. II, p. 218.

2. David Williams, "Voltaire: Literary Critic," *SVEC,* 48 (1966), p. 218.

3. Voltaire, *Works* (Fleming trans.), Vol. III, Pt. II, p. 63.

4. Ibid., p. 167.

5. R. S. Ridgway, *Voltaire and Sensibility* (Montreal: McGill-Queens University Press, 1973), p. 45.

6. "Urania" is another name for Aphrodite. See Ira Wade, "The Epitre à Uranie," *PMLA* 47 (Dec. 1932), pp. 1066-112.

7. Voltaire, *Works* (Fleming trans.), Vol. X, Pt. II, pp. 47–48.

8. Ibid., p. 48.

9. Ibid.

10. Ibid., p. 45.

11. Ibid., p. 54.

12. Ibid., p. 69.

13. See David Williams, *Voltaire: Literary Critic,* pp. 342-54.

14. See Raymond Naves, *Le Goût de Voltaire* (Paris: Garnier, 1938), p. 416.

15. Voltaire, *Works* (Fleming trans.), Vol. VII, Pt. II, p. 49.

16. Florence D. White, *Voltaire's Essay on Epic Poetry: A Study and an Edition* (New York: Phaeton Press, 1970), p. 83.

17. Ibid.

18. Ibid., pp. 90–92.
19. Ibid., p. 99
20. Ibid., p. 97.
21. Ibid., p. 107.
22. Ibid., p. 113.
23. Ibid., p. 131.
24. Ibid., p. 149.
25. Ibid.
26. Ibid., pp. 149–50.
27. Ibid., p. 150.
28. Ibid., Vol. XXI, Pt. II, p. 9.
29. Ibid., p. 10.
30. Ibid., Vol. XV, Pt. II, p. 62.
31. Ibid., p. 115.
32. R. S. Ridgway, *Voltaire and Sensibility*, p. 150.
33. Voltaire, *Works* (Fleming trans.), Vol. XV, Pt. I, pp. 105–06.
34. On "Le Mondain" see André Morize, *L'Apologie du luxe au XVIIIᵉ siècle: Le Mondain et ses sources* (Paris: Didier, 1909).
35. Voltaire, *Works* (Fleming trans.), Vol. I, Pt. II, p. 289.
36. Ibid.
37. Ibid., Vol. X, Pt. II, p. 187.
38. Ibid., Vol. I, Pt. I, p. 301.
39. Ibid., p. 297.
40. Ibid., Vol. X, Pt. II, p. 189.
41. Ibid., p. 25.
42. Ibid., p. 32.
43. Ibid., p. 34.
44. Ibid., p. 6.
45. Ibid., p. 17.
46. See George R. Havens, "Voltaire's Pessimistic Revision of his *Poème sur le désastre de Lisbonne*," *Modern Language Notes*, Vol. 44 (1929), pp. 489–92.
47. See Lilian Willens, "Voltaire's Comic Theatre," *SVEC*, 136 (1975); also R. S. Ridgway, *Voltaire and Sensibility*, pp. 197–221.
48. T. W. Russell, *Voltaire, Dryden and Heroic Tragedy* (New York: AMS Press, 1966), p. 2.
49. Ibid., pp. 10–65.
50. Voltaire, *Works* (Fleming trans.), Vol. XIX, Pt. II, p. 171.
51. Ibid.
52. R. S. Ridgway, *Voltaire and Sensibility*, p. 168.
53. Voltaire, *Works* (Fleming trans.), Vol. XIX, Pt. II, p. 160.
54. Ibid., p. 191.
55. T. W. Russell, *Voltaire, Dryden and Heroic Tragedy*, p. 95.
56. Voltaire, *Works* (Fleming trans.), Vol. XIX, Pt. I, p. 141.

57. See R. S. Ridgway, "La propagande philosophique dans les tragédies de Voltaire," *SVEC*, 15 (1961).

58. Voltaire, *Works*, Vol. IX, Pt. I, p. 61.

59. Ibid., p. 4.

60. Ibid.

61. Ibid., Vol. VIII, Pt. II, p. 11.

62. Ibid.

63. Ibid., Vol. IX, Pt. I, p. 4.

64. Ibid.

65. Ibid., Vol. VIII, Pt. II, p. 304.

66. Ibid., p. 312.

67. Jack R. Vrooman, "Voltaire's Theatre," *SVEC*, 75 (1970), p. 207.

68. See Robert A. Niklaus, *A Literary History of France: 1715–1789* (London: Ernest Benn, 1970), pp. 166–71.

69. R. S. Ridgway, *Voltaire and Sensibility*, pp. 170, 192.

70. Ralph A. Nablow, "A Study of Voltaire's Lighter Verse," *SVEC*, 126 (1974), pp. 282–83.

71. Voltaire, *Works* (Fleming trans.), Vol. X, Pt. II, p. 82.

72. See Theodore Besterman, *Voltaire* (New York: Harcourt, Brace and World, 1969), p. 339.

73. Ibid., p. 421.

74. Voltaire, *Works* (Fleming trans.), Vol. X, Pt. II, p. 237.

75. Ibid., p. 267.

76. See Theodore Besterman, *Voltaire*, p. 177.

77. Ibid., p. 173.

78. Ibid., p. 286.

79. See Voltaire, *Oeuvres critiques et poétiques*, edited by Roger Petit (Paris: Larousse, 1937), p. 101.

80. Ibid., p. 106.

Chapter Three

1. See Wade, *Intellectual Development*, p. 93–109.

2. J. H. Brumfitt, *Voltaire, Historian* (Oxford: Oxford University Press, 1958), p. 1.

3. Ibid., p. 47.

4. J. H. Brumfitt (trans.), *Voltaire, The Age of Louis XIV and Other Selected Writings* (New York: Washington Square Press, 1963), p. 318. Hereafter cited as Brumfitt, *Age of Louis XIV*.

5. Ibid., p. 331.

6. John B. Black, *The Art of History* (London: Methuen, 1926), p. 29.

7. Voltaire, *Works* (Fleming trans.), Vol. XIX, Pt. I, p. 269.

8. Brumfitt, *Age of Louis XIV*, p. 333.
9. Ibid.
10. Quoted in Richard Aldington, *Voltaire* (London: George Rout-ledge, 1925), p. 212.
11. Ferdinand Schevill, *Six Historians* (Chicago: Chicago University Press), 1956, p. 117.
12. Quoted by John B. Black, *The Art of History*, p. 29.
13. Brumfitt, *Age of Louis XIV*, p. 323.
14. Ibid., p. 324.
15. See Virgil W. Topazio, *Voltaire: A Critical Study* (New York: Random House), p. 160.
16. Voltaire, *Works* (Fleming trans.), Vol. XI, Pt. II, p. 8.
17. John B. Black, *The Art of History*, p. 64.
18. Ibid., p. 64.
19. Voltaire, *Works* (Fleming trans.), Vol. XI, Pt. I, pp. 171–72.
20. Best., *Corres.*, D1334 (c. 1 June 1737).
21. Voltaire, *Works* (Fleming trans.), Vol. XI, Pt. II, p. 46.
22. Lionel Gossman, "Voltaire's *Charles XII:* History Into Art," *SVEC*, 25 (1963), p. 691.
23. Voltaire, *Works* (Fleming trans.), Vol. XI, Pt. II, p. 47.
24. Ibid.
25. Ibid., p. 10.
26. Ibid.
27. Best., *Corres.* D1642 (30 October 1738).
28. Ibid.
29. Ibid., p. 181.
30. Voltaire, *Works* (Fleming trans.), Vol. XII, Pt. I, pp. 5–12.
31. Brumfitt, *Age of Louis XIV*, p. 122.
32. Ibid., p. 127.
33. Ibid.
34. Gustave Lanson, *Voltaire*, translated by R. A. Wagoner (New York: John Wiley, 1960), pp. 99–100.
35. John B. Black, *The Art of History*, p. 66.
36. Voltaire, *Works* (Fleming trans.), Vol. XII, Pt. II, p. 208.
37. Brumfitt, *Age of Louis XIV*, p. 145.
38. Voltaire, *Works* (Fleming trans.), Vol. XII, Pt. II, pp. 206–07.
39. Ibid.
40. William Church (ed.), *Louis XIV in Historical Thought* (New York: W. W. Norton, 1976), p. 114.
41. William Church (ed.), *The Greatness of Louis XIV* (Lexington, Mass., Heath, 1959), p. 297.
42. Voltaire, *Works* (Fleming trans.), Vol. XV, Pt. I, p. 127.
43. Condorcet, quoted in Voltaire, *Le siècle de Louis XIV*, ed. Roger Petit (Paris: Larousse, 1936), p. 125.

44. Quoted by Will and Ariel Durant, *The Age of Voltaire* (New York: Simon & Schuster, 1963), p. 488.

45. Voltaire, quoted in Paul Sakmann, *Three German Studies in Enlightenment Historiography* (Middletown, Conn.: Wesleyan University Press, 1971), p. 24.

46. See G. P. Gooch, "Catherine the Great and Voltaire" in his *Catherine the Great and Other Studies* (London: Longmans, Green, 1954).

47. John B. Black, *The Art of History*, p. 71.

48. Voltaire, *Works* (Fleming trans.), Vol. XIII, Pt. I, pp. 26–31.

49. Voltaire, *Works* (Fleming trans.), Vol. XV, Pt. II, pp. 194–95.

50. Ibid., p. 220.

51. Ibid., Vol. XIII, Pt. I, pp. 146–47.

52. Ibid., Vol. XV, Pt. II, p. 244.

53. Ibid., Vol. XIII, Pt. 1, pp. 178–79.

54. Ibid., Vol. XV, Pt. I, p. 105.

55. Ibid., Vol. XVI, Pt. I, pp. 133.

56. Ibid., p. 135.

57. Ibid., p. 144.

58. Brumfitt, *Age of Louis XIV*, p. 311.

59. Jerome Rosenthal, "Voltaire's Philosophy of History," *Journal of the History of Ideas*, XVI (April, 1955), p. 159.

60. Voltaire, *Works* (Fleming trans.), Vol. XVI, Pt. I, p. 250.

61. Paul K. Conkin and Roland N. Stromberg, *The Heritage and Challenge of History* (New York: Dodd, Mead, 1971), p. 49.

62. Michelet, quoted by Will and Ariel Durant, *The Age of Voltaire*, p. 489.

Chapter Four

1. Wade, *Intellectual Development*, p. 763.

2. Voltaire, *Works* (Fleming trans.), Vol. XXI, Pt. II, p. 9.

3. Peter Gay (ed.), *The Enlightenment* (New York: Simon & Schuster, 1973), p. 13.

4. Albert Guérard, *The Life and Death of an Ideal: France in the Classical Age* (New York: Braziller, 1956), p. 259.

5. Norman L. Torrey (ed.), *Les Philosophes* (New York: Capricorn, 1960), p. 10.

6. Peter Gay (ed.), *The Enlightenment*, p. 29.

7. Lytton Strachey, *Books and Characters* (New York: Harcourt Brace, 1922), p. 115; p. 133.

8. Voltaire, *Philosophical Letters*, translated by Ernest Dilworth (Indianapolis: Bobbs-Merrill Co., 1961), p. 64.

9. Ibid., p. 58.

10. See Wade, *Intellectual Development,* pp. 342–48.
11. Voltaire, *Philosophical Letters,* pp. 3–21.
12. Voltaire, *Works* (Fleming trans.), Vol. XIX, Pt. II, pp. 218–19.
13. Ibid., Vol. XIX, Pt. I, p. 91.
14. Ibid., p. 93.
15. Ibid., Vol. XIX, Pt. II, p. 45.
16. Ibid., p. 49.
17. Ibid., p. 175.
18. Voltaire, *Philosophical Letters,* p. 110.
19. Voltaire, *Works* (Fleming trans.), Vol. XIX, Pt. II, p. 6.
20. Ibid.
21. Ibid., Vol. XI, Pt. II, p. 212.
22. Ibid., pp. 221–22.
23. Ibid., p. 235.
24. Ibid.
25. See Voltaire, *Dernières remarques sur les pensées de M. Pascal* (1777), Moland, Vol. 31, pp. 1–40.
26. See Voltaire, *Traité de metaphysique,* Moland, Vol. 22, pp. 189–230.
27. Ibid., p. 194.
28. Ibid.
29. Ibid., pp. 196–97.
30. Ibid., pp. 201–15.
31. Ibid., p. 217.
32. Ibid., p. 225.
33. Ibid.
34. Voltaire, *Philosophical Dictionary,* ed. Peter Gay (New York: Basic Books, 1962), p. 3.
35. Father Léonce de Grandmaison, "La religion et l'irréligion de Voltaire," *Études* (Jan. 5, 1926), p. 12.
36. Father Bron, S. J., quoted in Kathleen O'Flaherty, *Voltaire: Myth and Reality,* 2nd ed. (Oxford: Blackwell, 1945), p. 5.
37. Voltaire, *Philosophical Dictionary,* ed. Peter Gay, p. 5.
38. Voltaire, *Works* (Fleming trans.), Vol. III, Pt. I, p. 53, p. 57.
39. Ibid., Vol. III, Part II, p. 244.
40. Ibid., Vol. IV, Pt. II, p. 49, p. 326.
41. Ibid., Vol. IV, Pt. I, pp. 20–21.
42. Ibid., Vol. III, Pt. I, p. 141.
43. Ibid., Vol. IV, Pt. I, p. 54.
44. Ibid.
45. Ibid., Vol. IV, Pt. II, p. 326.
46. Ibid., pp. 329–30.
47. Ibid., p. 326.
48. Ibid. Vol. VII, Pt. I, pp. 274–75.
49. Ibid., Vol. IV, Pt. I, p. 60.

50. Ibid.
51. Ibid.
52. Ibid., Vol. IV, Pt. II, p. 90.
53. Ibid., pp. 90–91.
54. Ibid.
55. Ibid.
56. Ibid., Vol. V, Pt. I, pp. 131–32.
57. Ibid., Vol. III, Pt. II, p. 112.
58. Ibid., p. 115.
59. Ibid., Vol. V, Pt. II, pp. 241–42.
60. Ibid., Vol. VII, Pt. I, pp. 84–85.
61. Ibid., Vol. XVIII, Pt. II, p. 240.
62. Ibid., p. 288.

Chapter Five

1. See Vivienne Mylne, "Literary Techniques and Methods in Voltaire's *contes philosophiques*," *SVEC*, 57 (1967), pp. 1055–80.
2. Condorcet, quoted in Pol Gaillard, *Candide* (Paris: Hatier, 1972), p. 78.
3. Voltaire, *Romans et Contes*, pres. par Henri Bernec, ed. Naves, (Paris: Garnier Frères, 1960), "Zadig," p. 3. Throughout our discussion of Voltaire's *contes* we have been indebted to our study of Jacques Van den Heuvel's *Voltaire dans ses contes* (Paris, Colin, 1967).
4. Voltaire, *Romans et Contes*, "Zadig," p. 7.
5. Ibid., p. 23.
6. Ibid., pp. 23–24.
7. Ibid., p. 38.
8. Ibid., pp. 41–42.
9. Ibid., p. 52.
10. Ibid., pp. 55–56.
11. Ibid., p. 56.
12. Ibid.
13. Ibid., "Micromégas," p. 97.
14. Ibid., p. 98.
15. Ibid.
16. Ibid., p. 108.
17. Ibid., p. 109.
18. Ibid., pp. 109–110.
19. Jean Sareil, *Essai sur Candide* (Genève: Droz, 1967), p. 30.
20. René Pomeau, *Voltaire par lui-même* (Paris: Editions du Seuil, 1955), p. 63.
21. Ira O. Wade, *The Structure and Form of the French Enlightenment* (Princeton: Princeton University Press, 1977), Vol. II, p. 35.

22. Voltaire, *Romans et Contes*, "Candide ou l'optimisme," p. 138.
23. Ibid.
24. Ibid., p. 216.
25. Ibid., pp. 189–90.
26. Ibid., p. 190.
27. Ira O. Wade, *Voltaire and Candide: A Study in the Fusion of History, Art and Philosophy* (Princeton: Princeton University Press, 1959), p. 319.
28. Voltaire, *Romans et Contes*, "Candide," p. 167.
29. Ibid., p. 173.
30. Ibid., p. 182.
31. Ibid., p. 199. An allusion to the execution in 1747 of the English admiral George Byng for losing a naval battle to the French. Previously Voltaire had unsuccessfully tried to save his life.
32. Ibid., p. 195.
33. Ibid., "L'Ingénu," p. 253.
34. Ibid., p. 262.
35. Ibid., p. 248.
36. Ibid., p. 261.
37. Ibid., p. 254.
38. Ibid., p. 273.
39. Ibid., p. 317.
40. Ibid.
41. Best., *Corres.* 13360 (June/July 1767).
42. Voltaire, *L'Ingénu*, pres. par Jean Varloot (Paris, Editions Sociales), p. 16.
43. Voltaire, quoted in Marius Roustan, *The Pioneers of the French Revolution* (London: Ernest Benn, 1926), p. 290.
44. Voltaire, *Works* (Fleming trans.), Vol. I, Pt. II, p. 144.
45. Ibid., Vol. II, Pt. II, p. 15.
46. Ibid., p. 17.
47. Ibid., p. 23.
48. Ibid., p. 27.
49. Ibid.
50. Ibid., p. 15.

Chapter Six

1. Ernest Bersot, quoted in Paul Harvey and J. E. Heseltine (eds.), *The Oxford Companion to French Literature* (Oxford: Clarendon Press, 1959), p. 756.
2. C. P. Snow, *The Two Cultures and A Second Look*, (Cambridge: Cambridge University Press, 1965).

3. Margaret S. Libby, *The Attitude of Voltaire to Magic and the Sciences* (New York: AMS Press, 1966), p. 12.

4. Ibid.

5. Moland, Vol. 35, p. 19.

6. Ibid., Vol. 37, p. 404.

7. Libby, *The Attitude of Voltaire to Magic and the Sciences*, p. 266.

8. Ibid., pp. 252–53.

9. Ibid., p. 253.

10. Moland, Vol. 41, p. 529.

11. Ibid., Vol. 43, p. 223.

12. J. Robert Oppenheimer, *Science and Common Sense* (New York: Simon & Schuster, 1953), p. 89.

13. Moland, Vol. 21, p. 219–20.

14. Voltaire, *"Candide," "Zadig," and Selected Stories*, translated by Donald M. Frame (Bloomington, Indiana: Indiana University Press, 1961), "Micromégas," p. 189.

15. Bertrand Russell, "Voltaire's Influence on Me," *SVEC*, Vol. VI (1958), p. 161.

16. Ibid.

17. Ibid., p. 162.

18. Voltaire, *Works* (Fleming trans.), Vol. VI, Pt. I, pp. 58–59.

19. That Voltaire's wit is still appreciated is evidenced by the large number of quotations in Evan Esar, *Dictionary of Humorous Quotations* (New York: Horizon Press, 1949), pp. 182–84 in which the illustrations in this section are found.

20. Voltaire, *"Candide," "Zadig," and Selected Stories* (translated by Donald M. Frame), p. 171.

21. Ibid., p. 16.

22. James W. Thompson and B. J. Holm, *History of Historical Writing* (New York: Macmillan, 1942), p. 66.

23. George R. Havens (ed.), *Voltaire's Candide ou l'optimisme* (New York: Holt, Rinehart & Winston, 1969), lxvii.

24. Eugène Ionesco, quoted in Martin Esslin, *Theatre of the Absurd* (New York: Anchor Books, 1961), xix.

25. Martin Esslin, *Theatre of the Absurd*, p. 301.

26. Albert Camus, *The Myth of Sisyphus and Other Essays* (translated by Justin O'Brien) (New York: Random House, 1955), p. 37.

27. Patrick Henry, "Voltaire and Camus: The Limits of Reason and Absurdity," *SVEC*, 138 (1975), p. 249.

28. Ibid., p. 251.

29. Ibid., p. 256.

30. Theodore C. Greening, "Candide: an Existentialist Dream," *Journal of Existentialism*, Vol. V (Summer 1965), p. 413.

31. George A. Perla, "Zadig, Hero of the Absurd," *SVEC*, 143 (1975), p. 52.

32. Merle L. Perkins, "Voltaire's Concept of International Order," *SVEC*, 5 (1965).

33. Ibid., p. 262.

34. Henry Meyer, "Voltaire on War and Peace," *SVEC*, 144 (1975), p. 192.

35. See Karl Popper, "Utopia and Violence," *Hibbert Journal*, Vol. XLVI (1947–1948), pp. 109–116.

36. Voltaire, quoted in Alfred O. Aldridge, *Voltaire and the Century of Light*, p. 413.

37. Paul Chaponnière, quoted in Norman L. Torrey, *The Spirit of Voltaire*, p. 216.

38. Voltaire, quoted in Renée Waldinger, *Voltaire and Reform in the Light of the French Revolution* (Nevene: Droz, 1959), p. 98.

39. Ibid., pp. 104–107.

40. Regnaud de Saint-Jean-D'Angely, quoted in Marius Roustan, *The Pioneers of the French Revolution* (London: Benn, 1926), p. 293.

41. Heine, quoted in Norman L. Torrey, *The Spirit of Voltaire*, p. 233.

42. See Otis Fellows, "Voltaire in Liberated France," *Romanic Review*, Vol. 37 (1946), pp. 168–76.

43. Ibid., pp. 169–70.

44. Ibid., p. 171.

45. Jimmy Carter, Inaugural Address, January 20, 1977.

46. Ibid.

47. Will and Ariel Durant, *The Age of Voltaire*, p. 786.

48. Paul Valéry, quoted in Otis Fellows, "Voltaire in Liberated France," p. 170.

49. The Chevalier de Boufflers, quoted in Norman L. Torrey, *The Spirit of Voltaire*, p. 1.

50. Lanson, quoted in Torrey, *The Spirit of Voltaire*, p. 1.

51. Harold J. Morovitz, "A Possible Remedy for Thinking That Leads Youth into Easy Acceptance of Cult Figures," *New York Times*, November 26, 1978.

52. Ibid.

53. André Delattre, *Voltaire L'impétueux* (Paris, Mercure de France, 1957), pp. 43–44.

54. Ibid., p. 101.

55. Paul Valéry, quoted in Robert M. Adams (ed.), *Candide or Optimism* (New York: W. W. Norton, 1968), p. 192.

56. Voltaire, quoted in Norman L. Torrey, *The Spirit of Voltaire*, p. 259.

Selected Bibliography

PRIMARY SOURCES

The Age of Louis XIV. Translated by M. P. Pollack. Everyman Library. London: J. M. Dent & Sons, 1926.

The Age of Louis XIV and Other Selected Writings. Translated and edited by J. H. Brumfitt. New York: Washington Square Press, 1963.

Candide (A Bilingual Edition). Translated and edited by Peter Gay. New York: St. Martin's Press, 1963.

"Candide" and Other Writings. Edited by Haskell M. Block. New York: Random House, 1956.

Candide or Optimism. Translated and edited by Robert M. Adams. New York: W. W. Norton & Company, 1966.

Candide, ou l'Optimisme. Edited by George R. Havens. New York: Holt, Rinehart & Winston, 1934.

Candide ou l'Optimisme. Edited by André Morize. Paris: Hachette, 1913.

Candide ou l'Optimisme. Edited by René Romeau. Paris: Nizet, 1959.

"Candide," "Zadig," and Selected Stories. Translated by Donald M. Frame. Bloomington: Indiana University Press, 1961.

Complete Works of Voltaire. Edited by Theodore Besterman. Genève: Institut et Musée Voltaire; Banbury: Voltaire Institute, 1968–.

Contes et romans. Edited by Philippe Van Tieghem. 4 vols. Paris: Roches, 1930.

The History of Charles XII. Translated by W. Todhunter. London: J. M. Dent & Sons, 1908.

The Living Thoughts of Voltaire, presented by André Maurois. New York: Longmans, Green, & Company, 1939.

Oeuvres complètes. Edited by Louis Moland. 52 vols. Paris: Garnier, 1877–1885.

Philosophical Dictionary. Translated and edited by Peter Gay. Preface by André Maurois. 2 vols. New York: Basic Books, 1962.

Philosophical Letters. Translated with an Introduction by Ernest Dilworth. Indianapolis: Bobbs-Merrill Co., 1961.

Politique de Voltaire. Edited by René Pomeau. Paris: Colin, 1963.

The Portable Voltaire. Edited by Ben Ray Redman. New York: The Viking Press, 1957.

Select Letters of Voltaire. Translated and edited by Theodore Bester-
man. London: Thomas Nelson & Sons, 1963.
The Selected Letters of Voltaire. Edited and translated by Richard A.
Brooks. New York: New York University Press, 1973.
Selections from Voltaire. Edited by George R. Havens. Revised edi-
tion. New York: Holt, Rinehart & Winston, 1969.
Voltaire and the Enlightenment: Selections from Voltaire. Translated
by Norman L. Torrey. New York: Appleton-Century-Crofts, 1931.
Voltaire on Religion: Selected Writings. Translated and edited by Ken-
neth W. Applegate. New York: Frederick Ungar, 1974.
Voltaire's Correspondence. Edited by Theodore Besterman. 107 vols.
Genève: Institut et Musée Voltaire, 1953–1965.
Voltaire's Essay on Epic Poetry: A Study and an Edition. Edited by
Florence D. White. New York: Phaeton Press, 1970.
Voltaire's Notebooks. Edited by Theodore Besterman. 2 vols. Genève:
Institut et Musée Voltaire, 1952.
The Works of Voltaire. Translated by William F. Fleming and others.
22 vols. New York: The St. Hubert Guild, 1901.

SECONDARY SOURCES

1. Bibliographies

BARR, MARY-MARGARET H. *A Century of Voltaire Study; a Bibliography of Writing on Voltaire, 1825–1925.* New York: Institute
of French Studies, 1929.
———— and FREDERICK A. SPEAR. *Quarante années d'études Voltair-
iennes: Bibliographie analytique des livres et articles sur Voltaire,
1926–1965.* Paris: Colin, 1968.
BENGESCO, GEORGES. *Voltaire: Bibliographie de ses oeuvres.* 4 vols.
Rouveyre and Blond (Vol. 1), Perrin (Vols. 2–4), 1882–90. (To
be used in conjunction with Malcolm *Table* listed below).
BROOKS, RICHARD A. and others. *A Critical Bibliography of French
Literature.* Vol. IV, *Supplement, The Eighteenth Century,* Chap.
VII on Voltaire, pp. 113–41. Syracuse: Syracuse University
Press, 1968.
CABEEN, DAVID C. and others. *A Critical Bibliography of French
Literature.* Vol. IV, *The Eighteenth Century,* Chap. VII on
Voltaire, pp. 182–207. Volume editors: George R. Havens, Donald
F. Bond and others. Syracuse: Syracuse University Press, 1951.
EVANS, HYWEL BERWYN. *A Provisional Bibliography of English Edi-
tions and Translations of Voltaire.* Vol. 9, pp. 9–121, in *Studies
on Voltaire and the Eighteenth Century.* Genève: Institut et
Musée Voltaire, 1959.

MALCOLM, JEAN. *Table de la bibliographie de Voltaire par Bengesco.* Genève: Institut et Musée Voltaire, 1953.

2. Books

ALDINGTON, RICHARD. *Voltaire.* London: Routledge & Kegan Paul, 1925. Interesting though somewhat superficial survey of Voltaire's life, thought, and literary works.

ALDRIDGE, ALFRED O. *Voltaire and the Century of Light.* Princeton: Princeton University Press, 1975. A recent biographical study of Voltaire based firmly on the correspondence and new sources.

BESTERMAN, THEODORE. *Voltaire.* New York: Harcourt, Brace & World, 1969. Detailed but somewhat disappointing biography by a dominant figure in twentieth-century Voltairian scholarship. Appendix contains "Voltaire's Autobiography."

————. *Voltaire Essays and Another.* London: Oxford University Press, 1962. Eleven lucidly written essays on subjects ranging from Flaubert's judgment of Voltaire to Houdon's statue of him.

————. Founder and editor of *Studies on Voltaire and the Eighteenth Century* (1955–present). Genève: Institut et Musée Voltaire, 1955–1970; Oxford: The Voltaire Foundation, since 1971 (present editor, H. T. Mason). Major source for articles and monographs in French and English on Voltaire and French literature of his time.

BOTTIGLIA, WILLIAM F. "Voltaire's *Candide:* Analysis of a Classic," 2nd ed. *Studies on Voltaire and the Eighteenth Century.* Genève: Institut et Musée Voltaire, 1964. A painstaking examination of Candide—its background, structure, and content.

————, ed. *Voltaire, a Collection of Critical Essays.* Englewood Cliffs, N.J.: Prentice-Hall, 1968. An excellent sampling of the best critical opinions on various aspects of Voltaire's life and works.

BRAILSFORD, HENRY N. *Voltaire.* New York: Holt, Rinehart & Winston, 1935. Uncritical but highly readable account of Voltaire the reformer and precursor of the French Revolution.

BRANDES, GEORGE. *Voltaire.* 2 vols. New York: 1930. Interesting and extensive analysis of Voltaire as man, artist, and reformer by an outstanding Danish critic.

BRUMFITT, JOHN H. *Voltaire Historian.* Oxford: Oxford University Press, 1958. Discusses Voltaire's predecessors in historiography, and surveys and evaluates his historical works.

CASSIRER, ERNST. *The Philosophy of the Enlightenment.* Translated by Fritz C. A. Koelin and James P. Pettegrove. Princeton: Princeton University Press, 1959. A difficult but indispensable study of the philosophical foundations of the period. Emphasizes German thought.

182

CAUSSY, FERNAND. *Voltaire seigneur de village.* Paris: Hachette, 1912. Thorough study of Voltaire in his roles as patriarch, reformer, and administrator at Ferney in his later life.

DELATTRE, ANDRÉ. *Voltaire L'impétueux.* Paris: Mercure de France, 1957. Psychological interpretation of Voltaire's character, his inner struggles and repressions. Provocative but one-sided.

DESNOIRESTERRES, GUSTAVE. *Voltaire et la société française au XVIIIe siècle.* 2nd ed. 8 vols. Paris: Didier, 1867–1876. An invaluable storehouse of information on Voltaire's life, times, and works.

DURANT, WILL and ARIEL. *The Age of Voltaire. The Story of Civilization,* Vol. 9. New York: Simon & Schuster, 1965. Popular account of Voltaire's life and times within panoramic view of whole period.

———. *Rousseau and Revolution. The Story of Civilization.* Vol. X. New York: Simon & Schuster, 1967. Contains highly readable account of Voltaire's final years and influence.

FOSTER, MILTON P., ed. *Voltaire's Candide and the Critics.* Belmont, California: Wadsworth Publishing Company, 1964. Wide variety of materials to enhance the study of Voltaire's masterpiece—its background, form, content, and reception by critics. Contains translation of text by Donald M. Frame.

GAILLARD, POL. *Candide: Analyse Critique.* Paris: Hatier, 1972. Brief critical analysis of the *conte's* structure, content, and contemporary relevance.

GAY, PETER. *The Enlightenment: An Interpretation.* 2 vols. New York: Alfred Knopf, 1966. Volume 1 of this comprehensive study contains an excellent chapter on *Candide* (pp. 197–203).

———. *Voltaire's Politics: the Poet as Realist.* Princeton: Princeton University Press, 1959. Penetrating study of Voltaire's political theories as related to his practical political experience. Focuses on Voltaire's defense of monarchism.

GUIRAGOSSIAN, DIANA. *Voltaire's Facéties.* Genève, Librarie Droz, 1963. Excellent brief study of Voltaire's often neglected shorter pieces, emphasizing their role in his struggle with his and the *philosophes'* enemies.

HAVENS, GEORGE R. *The Age of Ideas.* New York: Henry Holt & Company, 1955. Well-written and reliable account of Voltaire's life and work included in a brilliant reconstruction of the French Enlightenment.

HENRY, PATRICK. "Voltaire and Camus: the Limits of Reason and the Awareness of Absurdity." Vol. 138 in *Studies on Voltaire and the Eighteenth Century.* Banbury: The Voltaire Foundation, 1975. Brilliant comparison of existentialist themes in two seemingly quite different authors.

LANSON, GUSTAVE. *Voltaire.* Translated by Robert A. Wagoner. New

York: John Wiley & Sons, 1966. Considered by many scholars to be the best single book on Voltaire. Recent Voltairian scholarship discussed in appendix by René Pomeau.

LIBBY, MARGARET SHERWOOD. *The Attitude of Voltaire to Magic and the Sciences.* New York: AMS Press, 1966. A somewhat dated but still fascinating discussion of Voltaire's knowledge and opinions on the biological and physical sciences, medicine, and magic.

MASON, HAYDN. *Voltaire.* New York: St. Martin's Press, 1975. Sound study of Voltaire in his various aspects.

MAUROIS, ANDRÉ. *Voltaire.* Translated by Hamish Miles. New York: Appleton-Century, 1938. A glowing but not particularly original appreciation of Voltaire by a modern French master.

McGHEE, DOROTHY M. *Voltairian Narrative Devices as Considered in the Author's Contes Philosophiques.* Menasha, Wisconsin: George Banta Publishing Company, 1933. Helpful analyses of Voltaire's stories, focusing on plot structure.

MITFORD, NANCY. *Voltaire in Love.* New York: Harper & Row, 1957. Not a biography but a lively and fascinating account of Voltaire's relationship with Mme du Châtelet.

MORLEY, JOHN. *Voltaire.* London: Macmillan & Company, 1913. Old (1872) but still valuable assessment by a brilliant Englishman of Voltaire's life, works, and influence.

NABLOW, RALPH A. "A Study of Voltaire's Lighter Verse." Vol. 126 in *Studies on Voltaire and the Eighteenth Century.* Banbury: The Voltaire Foundation, 1974. An informative and well-balanced reconsideration of the poetry upon which Voltaire's claim to be a genuine poet rests.

NAVES, RAYMOND. *Le Goût de Voltaire.* Paris: Garnier, 1938. Extensive survey of the origin and development of Voltaire's taste as a literary critic and aesthetician.

————. *Voltaire, l'homme et l'oeuvre.* Paris: Boivin, 1942. Succinct and vivid account of Voltaire's life and work, stressing the essential unity of his thought.

NOYES, ALFRED. *Voltaire.* London: Faber & Faber, 1936. Interprets Voltaire as an essentially Christian moralist in his lifelong struggle for justice, peace, and tolerance.

PAPPAS, JOHN. *Voltaire and d'Alembert.* Bloomington: Indiana University Press, 1962. Brief and able study of two fellow encyclopaedists.

PARTON, JAMES. *Life of Voltaire.* 2 vols. Boston: Houghton Mifflin Company, 1882. An old but still readable biography broad in scope and rich in detail.

PERKINS, MERLE L. "Voltaire's Concept of International Order." Vol. 36 in *Studies on Voltaire and the Eighteenth Century.* Genève: Institut et Musée Voltaire, 1965. Thorough examination of Voltaire's views on European politics, international law, war and peace with emphasis on their relevance today.

POMEAU, RENÉ. *La Religion de Voltaire.* Paris: Nizet, 1956. A major detailed study of Voltaire's views on religion and of the development of his deism.

————. *Voltaire par lui-même.* Paris: Editions du seuil, 1955. Delightful and convincing portrait of Voltaire himself through carefully culled and edited selections from his works. Profusely illustrated.

PRICE, WILLIAM RALEIGH. *The Symbolism of Voltaire's Novels with Special Reference to "Zadig."* New York: Columbia University Press, 1911. Suggestive but not always convincing interpretation of Voltaire's use of symbols in his *contes philosophiques.*

PRINZ, BERNARD, ed. *Voltaire.* Paris: Hatier, 1973. A refreshing new look at Voltaire's views on good and evil, politics, religion, and ethics. A *Thema* anthology.

RIDGWAY, RONALD S. "La propagande philosophique dans les tragédies de Voltaire." Vol. 15 in *Studies on Voltaire and the Eighteenth Century.* Genève: Institut et Musée Voltaire, 1961. Interesting discussion and evaluation of Voltaire's theater as a vehicle for propagandizing his views as a *philosophe.*

————. *Voltaire and Sensibility.* Montreal and London: McGill-Queen's University Press, 1973. A masterly and eminently readable study of Voltaire as a man of feeling as revealed in his poetry, dramas, and prose. Epilogue on Voltaire and the Romantics.

RUSSELL, TRUSTEN WHEELER. *Voltaire, Dryden and Heroic Tragedy.* New York: AMS Press, 1966. Excellent study of English and French critical opinions on dramatic poetry which influenced Voltaire's theory and practice as a dramatist. Emphasis on comparisons of Voltaire's and Dryden's dramas.

SAINTSBURY, GEORGE. "Voltaire." *Encyclopaedia Britannica.* 11th ed. 1911. A superb brief study of Voltaire's literary achievements by a great modern literary critic.

SAREIL, JEAN. *Essai sur Candide.* Genève: Droz, 1967. A brilliant fresh look at *Candide* which emphasizes its essential humanism.

————. *Voltaire et la critique.* Englewood Cliffs, N.J.: Prentice-Hall, 1966. Well-chosen essays on Voltaire as a man, poet, critic, historian, *philosophe, conteur,* and propagandist.

TOPAZIO, VIRGIL W. *Voltaire: A Critical Study of His Major Works.* New York: Random House, 1967. One of the most successful attempts to survey Voltaire's works as a whole. Incisive, reliable, and readable.

TORREY, NORMAN L., ed. *Les Philosophes: The Philosophers of the Enlightenment and Modern Democracy.* New York, Capricorn

Books, 1960. Useful work on period. Contains selections from Voltaire (pp. 52–82; 233–83) with good introductions.
————. *The Spirit of Voltaire.* New York: Columbia University Press, 1938. Still ranks as one of the best assessments of Voltaire as a human being who despite his flaws and foibles was motivated by an intense love of humanity. Especially good on Voltaire's deism, mysticism, and humanism.
———— and OTIS FELLOWS, eds. *The Age of Enlightenment.* 2nd ed. New York: Meredith Corporation, 1971. First-rate introductions, selections from French sources, and notes.

VALÉRY, PAUL. *Voltaire.* Paris: Gallimard, 1957. An appreciation of Voltaire's topicality; delivered after the liberation of France in 1945.

VAN DEN HEUVEL, JACQUES. *Voltaire dans ses contes.* Paris: Colin, 1967. The definitive scholarly work on Voltaire's *contes* in relation to his life and thought.
————. "Voltaire", pp. 711–28 in Vol. III of *Histoire des littératures, Encyclopédie de la Pléiade.* Paris: Gallimard, 1958.

VROOMAN, JACK R. "Voltaire's Theatre: the Cycle from *Oedipe* to *Mérope.*" Vol. 75 in *Studies on Voltaire and the Eighteenth Century.* Genève: Institut et Musée Voltaire, 1970. A much-needed and able reevaluation of Voltaire's achievements as a dramatist.

WADE, IRA O. *The Intellectual Development of Voltaire.* Princeton: Princeton University Press, 1969. A monumental study of Voltaire's intellectual biography, it attempts to penetrate into the inner reality of the man.
————. *Voltaire and "Candide": A Study of the Fusion of History, Art, and Philosophy.* Princeton: Princeton University Press, 1959. An exhaustive and enlightening treatment of *Candide*'s philosophical background, genesis, and essential meaning. Includes text of La Vallière Manuscript of *Candide.*
————. *Voltaire's "Micromégas": A Study of the Fusion of Science, Myth, and Art.* Princeton: Princeton University Press, 1950. A careful and imaginative study of the first of Voltaire's *contes philosophiques* viewed as an incorporation in art form of Voltaire's humanistic philosophy of life. Includes annotated text of *Micromégas.*
————. *The Structure and Form of the French Enlightenment.* 2 vols. Princeton: Princeton University Press, 1977. Volume II (*Esprit révolutionnaire*) of this gigantic study of the inner unity of the Enlightenment contains a penetrating discussion of organic unity in Voltaire.

WALDINGER, RENÉE. *Voltaire and Reform in the Light of the French*

Revolution. Nevène: Droz, 1959. Generally reliable account of the evolution of Voltaire's attitude toward reform and of the attitude of French revolutionaries toward him.

WILLIAMS, DAVID. "Voltaire: Literary Critic." Vol. 48 in *Studies on Voltaire and the Eighteenth Century.* Genève: Institut et Musée Voltaire, 1966. A fine study of Voltaire's literary criticism in light of its seventeenth-century background.

3. Articles

Europe. May, 1959. Special number devoted to Voltaire.

FELLOWS, OTIS. "Voltaire in liberated France." *Romanic Review,* Vol. 37 (1946), pp. 168–76. Recounts how France celebrated its liberation with eulogies to Voltaire.

GREENING, THOMAS C. "*Candide:* An Existential Dream." *Journal of Existentialism,* Vol. V (Summer, 1965), pp. 413–16. *Candide* viewed as an attempt to find meaning in a world rife with evil and suffering.

HAVENS, GEORGE R. "The Nature Doctrine of Voltaire." *PMLA,* Vol. XL (December, 1925), pp. 852–62). Traces the development of Voltaire's tendency to identify the law of nature with the law of God.

———. "Candide Returns." *Diderot Studies* 16 (1973), pp. 347–59. Considers some recent interpretations of *Candide.*

JAMES, E. D. "Voltaire on the Nature of the Soul." *French Studies,* Vol. XXXII (January, 1978). Traces the development of Voltaire's thought on the nature of the soul and discusses the philosophical difficulties he encountered.

LEE, PATRICK. "Voltaire as Moralist." *Journal of the History of Ideas,* Vol. XXXVIII (January-March, 1977), pp. 141–46. Rejects the view that Voltaire is a philosopher.

ROSENTHAL, JEROME. "Voltaire's Philosophy of History." *Journal of the History of Ideas,* Vol. XVI (1955), pp. 151–78. Interprets Voltaire as primarily a moralist and propagandist of enlightenment in his writing of history.

La Table Ronde. Vol. 122 (February, 1958). Entire issue devoted to Voltaire.

TOPAZIO, VIRGIL W. "Voltaire, Philosopher of Human Progress." *PMLA,* Vol. 74 (September, 1959), pp. 356–64. Voltaire viewed appreciatively as a constructive thinker.

WADE, IRA O. "Voltaire's Name." *PMLA,* Vol. 44 (1929), pp. 546–64. Survey of various theories of the origin of the name "Voltaire" and Arouet's reasons for choosing it.

Index

FEB 19'87			

THIS IS NOT THE DATE DUE
SEE INSIDE FRONT COVER